How to Read Karl Barth's Church Dogmatics in One Book

How to Read Karl Barth's Church Dogmatics in One Book

A Sequential Guide to His Magnum Opus

DANIEL CHITRADA

RESOURCE *Publications* • Eugene, Oregon

HOW TO READ KARL BARTH'S CHURCH DOGMATICS IN ONE BOOK
A Sequential Guide to His Magnum Opus

Copyright © 2025 Daniel Chitrada. All rights reserved. Except for brief quotations in critical publications or reviews, no part of this book may be reproduced in any manner without prior written permission from the publisher. Write: Permissions, Wipf and Stock Publishers, 199 W. 8th Ave., Suite 3, Eugene, OR 97401.

Resource Publications
An Imprint of Wipf and Stock Publishers
199 W. 8th Ave., Suite 3
Eugene, OR 97401

www.wipfandstock.com

PAPERBACK ISBN: 979-8-3852-5578-8
HARDCOVER ISBN: 979-8-3852-5579-5
EBOOK ISBN: 979-8-3852-5580-1

08/28/25

To my esteemed professor, George Hunsinger,
who ignited and cultivated in me the essence of theology
within the illuminating context of Karl Barth

Contents

Preface | ix
Acknowledgments | xi
Introduction | xiii

The Doctrine of the Word of God (Vol. I/1) | 1
Chapter 1: The Word of God as the Criterion of Dogmatics | 5
Chapter 2: The Revelation of God | 14

The Doctrine of the Word of God (Vol. I/2) | 21
Chapter 2: The Revelation of God | 23
Chapter 3: Holy Scripture | 30
Chapter 4: The Proclamation of the Church | 33

The Doctrine of God (Vol. II/1) | 37
Chapter 5: The Knowledge of God | 39
Chapter 6: The Reality of God | 43

The Doctrine of God (Vol. II/2) | 47
Chapter 7: The Election of God | 49
Chapter 8: The Command of God | 53

CONTENTS

The Doctrine of Creation (Vol. III/1) | 57
Chapter 9: The Work of Creation | 59

The Doctrine of Creation (Vol. III/2) | 67
Chapter 10: The Creature | 69

The Doctrine of Creation (Vol. III/3) | 77
Chapter 11: The Creator and His Creature | 79

The Doctrine of Creation (Vol. III/4) | 85
Chapter 12: The Command of God the Creator | 87

The Doctrine of Reconciliation (Vol. IV.1) | 95
Chapter 13: The Subject-Matter and Problems of the Doctrine of Reconciliation | 97
Chapter 14: Jesus Christ, the Lord as Servant | 100

The Doctrine of Reconciliation (Vol. IV.2) | 109
Chapter 15: Jesus Christ, the Servant as Lord | 111

The Doctrine of Reconciliation (Vol. IV.3, First Half) | 119
Chapter 16: Jesus Christ, the True Witness | 121

The Doctrine of Reconciliation (Vol. IV.3, Second Half) | 125

The Doctrine of Reconciliation (Vol. IV.4—Fragment) | 130

Bibliography | 133

Preface

Karl Barth is widely regarded as one of the most significant theologians in the history of Christian theology, and his magnum opus, Church Dogmatics (CD), requires no introduction. Even though many of us appreciate the CD, only a few could summon the courage to read through all the volumes of the dogmatics to grasp the depth and breadth of his theology. This is because the extensive writing (CD) can overwhelm us from the inception of the thought itself. This closely aligns with my experience during my attempts to engage with the material a few years ago. I endeavored to locate supplementary texts that could encapsulate the fundamental arguments and principles of dogmatics within a single volume. Notwithstanding the abundance of writings on the CD, I found it arduous to extract the comprehensive essence of a solitary publication. This has led me to write, *How to Read Karl Barth's Church Dogmatics in One Book: A Sequential Guide to His Magnum Opus.*

This book offers a comprehensive overview of the subject matter covered in the CD. It encapsulates Barth's key arguments in succinct sentences, knitting them into the essence of the larger picture. Engaging with this text will enlighten you on the prominent themes and fundamental arguments presented throughout the CD. It extensively uses T&T Clark's edition of CD, which has been generously cited throughout to give a sense of reading the CD itself. I have utilized the German paragraphs (§) as headings to adhere closely to Barth's original German style and provide the

PREFACE

reader with a concise argument that navigates the deep ocean of CD. I presume this methodology will assist you in comprehending the key argument presented in each paragraph, enabling the reader to complete all volumes of the dogmatics within a single book.

    The book does not offer itself as a replacement for engaging with the CD; rather, its purpose is to inspire readers to approach the CD with guidance provided through this book. I have made a concerted effort to adhere closely to the English translation of the CD in order to assist you in developing a responsible familiarity with the writing style, which I anticipate will ultimately aid in your engagement with the CD. Additionally, I have employed gender-inclusive language, with the exception of direct quotations from Barth's statements.

    Engaging with the CD fosters profound confidence among lay Christians, clergy, and seminarians alike in our quest for the Kingdom of God. However, efforts to confine the whole CD within the parameters of a singular doctrine may hinder our understanding and appreciation of the rich work. Instead, I propose that through this book, we navigate alongside Barth in following the vessel of CD, traversing the vast ocean of God's love, guided by an undercurrent of mystery, which ultimately places us in the lap of Jesus Christ, the Word.

    DANIEL CHITRADA
    Fall 2025

Acknowledgments

I wish to convey my profound gratitude to Princeton Theological Seminary, which has played a pivotal role in deepening my understanding of Karl Barth's theology through its esteemed faculty and extensive resources, ultimately facilitating the creation of this book. I deeply appreciate Dr. Cleophus J. LaRue Jr.'s guidance and unwavering support in this endeavor. I extend my heartfelt appreciation to Resource Publications, an imprint of Wipf and Stock Publishers, for their exemplary assistance throughout the process of bringing this book to fruition. Additionally, I would like to acknowledge my beloved wife, Sarjana Chitrada, who has been my silent supporter and a persistent source of solace during tumultuous times, accompanying me on my journey with this book. Lastly, I thank my astounding professor, George Hunsinger, who laid a foundational stone in my pursuit of Karl Barth's theology, for which I will remain indebted for the rest of my life. This book is dedicated to him as a gesture of gratitude.

Introduction

Many years ago, when I first engaged with a segment of Church Dogmatics (CD), the initial journey, which commenced vibrantly, quickly became adrift in the profound ocean of his theology, unable to grasp even the surface of the theme I was perusing. This may be a common occurrence for those who begin reading CD without familiarity with the style of Barth's writings, which are characterized by small dialectical spirals that ultimately lead to larger themes. Indeed, each paragraph of CD conveys a distinct point, and one requires a great deal of patience to extract its essence and continue along the journey.

A close reading of CD has helped me muse and discover the specific focus in each volume that is more suitable for specific readers (I do not intend to suggest that Barth himself wrote with such emphasis). These focuses are mentioned as follows.

Volume one appears to represent a pastoral volume (if I may say), establishing the discipline of dogmatics in its service to the church and introducing the groundbreaking theology of the threefold form of the Word of God: revelation, scripture, and church proclamation, alongside its robust inseparability from the work of the Holy Spirit. Barth acknowledges the centrality of the Trinitarian God as the foundation of all theology and reiterates the mission of the church to engage in preaching and administering the sacraments, consistent with the principles espoused by the Reformers. Lastly, he advocates for a direction for dogmatics that penetrates both the ecclesial and ethical realms, with its functions as a hearing and teaching church.

Volume two addresses theological discourses on God's knowledge, asserting that God's true knowledge is fundamentally rooted in the revelation of Jesus Christ. This self-revelation in Christ diverges from natural theology, which presents itself as an independent revelation distinct from God's revelation. Barth also elaborates on the scope of this knowledge, asserting that it finds its inception and consummation in God's freedom. Furthermore, he discusses the divine perfections of grace, holiness, mercy, and righteousness as inherently inseparable from God's being, which is fully manifested in Jesus Christ. He advocates for a Christocentric understanding of predestination by positing that Jesus embodies both the electing God and the elected human, transcending every human rejection. Consequently, God in Christ transforms sinners into bearers of grace, affirming Jesus Christ as the ultimate divine revelation and will.

Volumes three and four present a thorough exploration intended for a lay audience (if I may say) regarding creation, which acquires its significance as the theatre of God's grace and covenantal purpose when perceived solely through the lens of Christ. He further advocates for the distinctiveness of human beings as female and male, and emphasizes the Sabbath as a symbol of human liberation from toil. Barth proposes the concept of evil as rooted in nothingness that was not called forth, remains a threat until the final redemption. But the sin and fallenness are overcome by grace. Additionally, he speaks in favor of ethics grounded in divine command and underscores the intrinsic value of human life in its interconnectedness with the vocation that embodies gratitude.

In the fourth volume, Barth expands the scope of his theological perspective by affirming the theology of reconciliation as a divine act, delineating Christ's dual role as both servant and Lord. He underscores Christ's prophetic work as a decisive victory over human falsehood. Furthermore, he identifies an inseparable unity between justification and sanctification. Ultimately, he establishes reconciliation as a Trinitarian act, manifested through the Father's election, the Son's mediation, and the Spirit's application in the world.

The Doctrine of the Word of God (Vol. I/1)

INTRODUCTION

1. The Task of Dogmatics

Barth commences the initial section of volume one by recognizing that dogmatics constitutes a theological discipline that serves the church in two principal ways:

1. Through the actions of individual believers.
2. Through the fellowship's proclamation via. preaching and the administration of sacraments.

The objective of theology is to perpetually revise and critique its discourse regarding God. Barth contends that while theology serves as a guiding principle, it remains fallible and must submit to the obedience of God's grace.[1] In other words, theology lacks any exclusive keys to knowledge aside from accepting the possibility of grace and affirming its claims.

He positions the discipline of theology as the foremost priority in the quest for human truth. While other sciences may also seek truth, it follows that all sciences must ultimately converge upon theology. Theology serves as the fundamental principle guiding all truth-seeking efforts, indicating that theology cannot be confined

---

1. Barth, *Church Dogmatics* I/1, 4; hereafter cited as I/1.

to scientific standards (I/1, 10). The dogmatics presuppose God in Jesus Christ as the essence of the church, making divine knowledge accessible to dogmatics (I/1, 12). "Christian speech," Barth writes, "must be tested by its conformity to Christ" (I/1, 13). The task of dogmatics is not to echo the apostles and prophets but to articulate what we voice on this basis.

Barth perceives dogmatics as the fundamental function of the church, which can be accomplished solely through an act of faith within the church of Jesus Christ. It is through God's gracious calling that individuals come to recognize faith as a pivotal element in all their endeavors. And the true dogmatics consistently pertain to God's gracious choice.

2. The Task of Prolegomena to Dogmatics

Barth presents prolegomena as a specific approach to observing, contemplating, comprehending, and evaluating the nature of knowledge within dogmatics. He notes that, in humanity, there exists a consistent point of contact for divine messages and a pursuit of God, regardless of the presence of sin in individuals by nature. Nevertheless, Barth highlights the imperative to reject a certain type of prolegomena for three key reasons. Firstly, it is to be dismissed owing to its lack of theological foundations. Secondly, it encompasses intricate issues that may lead to the neglect of the dogmatic endeavor itself. Lastly, it demonstrates a lack of circumspection in adequately addressing the notions of responsibility and relevance.

In the discourse surrounding apologetics and polemics, Barth contends that these methodologies for defending the faith are ineffective for three primary reasons. Firstly, he asserts that faith necessitates an ongoing struggle with unbelief, rather than being a singular occurrence. Secondly, he notes that apologetics and polemics can potentially divert attention from the fundamental issues pertaining to dogmatics. Lastly, he argues that these approaches frequently fail to interact with unbelief in a consistent and substantive manner once their immediate objectives have been achieved. Consequently, apologetics and polemics are regarded as superficial occurrences that undermine the essence of faith. In other words, the disciplines of apologetics and polemics lack a comprehensive approach to Christian life compared to dogmatics.

Chapter 1

The Word of God as the Criterion of Dogmatics

3. Church Proclamation as the Material of Dogmatics

In establishing the framework for the discipline of dogmatics, Barth underscores that human communication must invariably reflect the communication of God in principle. God actively unites individuals within the visible Church, and Jesus Christ serves as the embodiment of the church, sanctifying its discourse as God's. He posits that authentic Christian love constitutes the foundational element of the church's proclamation. Barth writes, "Proclamation (. . .) is its presupposition, its material and its practical goal, not its content or task" (I/1, 51). And human proclamation is not the Word of God but instead points to the prior utterance of God himself. Rhetorically, he voices proclamation as praise, active love, instruction, and theology.

    He further posits that the church cannot assert itself as the master of the Word; rather, its duty of proclamation must point to God's unmerited grace. "God may speak to us through a pagan or an atheist, and thus give us to understand that the boundary between the church and the secular world can still take at any time a different course from that which we think we discern" (I/1, 55).

According to Barth, the church's mandate of proclamation may be interpreted in two distinct ways:

1. Its commandment rooted in faith, hope, and love.
2. Its commission expressed through preaching and sacrament.

Consequently, the church derives its power of proclamation from the Word of God itself.

Barth then shifts his focus to admonishing the Roman Catholic Church as an institution of sacrament that failed to highlight the means of grace as essential for the church's vitality. He critiques the Church dogmaticians for neglecting the necessity of the preaching office, concentrating solely on the teaching office and its legitimate doctrines. Consequently, the Church has failed to produce any notable preachers in the past and present.

He subsequently articulates his rationale for proclamation by asserting, "Proclamation must mean repetition of the divine promise" (I/1, 67). God's presence embodies grace, encompassing the dual facets of receiving and responding to the promise with obedience. On one hand, proclamation is conceived as God functioning as the author, while on the other hand, it represents the foundational essence within the human individual. In this context, Barth delineates a critical contrast, recognizing that the Reformers perceived proclamation not in terms of a cause-and-effect relationship, as upheld by the Roman Catholic Church, but rather as an interplay between the Word and faith.

The church and its message must not compromise with scientific or aesthetic culture; rather, its duty is to serve God through proclamation. It is asserted that dogmatics and the church proclamation maintain a responsible relationship, wherein the former derives raw materials from the latter. And the function or task of dogmatics is to critically examine the church's proclamation, necessitating ongoing self-assessment. Consequently, dogmatics serve as a proper guide for the church's proclamation.

Barth advises that we should remain vigilant regarding the prayers and hymns of the church, as these may be impactful yet potentially distorted declarations. To remedy this situation, he delineates three essential guidelines. Firstly, dogmatics ought to function as a proclamation that has undergone rigorous evaluation, reflection, investigation, and amendment. Secondly, dogmatics should facilitate the church's proclamation by establishing a connection between faith and knowledge. Lastly, it is imperative for dogmatics to uphold the theme inherent in the church's proclamation. Thus, dogmatics not only encompasses the contents of preaching but also provides guidelines for correcting human speech, prayer, and hymns.

4. The Word of God in Its Threefold Form

Barth begins this section by observing the inseparability of the church and proclamation with the bread and wine in the communion that takes place simply and visibly. He analyzes the genuine or authentic proclamation in four concentric circles for prolegomena and dogmatics. The first outer circle encompasses humanity's discourse concerning God as directed by God. The second circle points to humans' discussion of God's self-objectification in the freedom of his grace in accordance with his good pleasure. The third inner circle interprets God as the determinant of virtue in the proclamation, serving simultaneously as its subject and object, necessitating attentive reception and appropriate compliance. Ultimately, the true proclamation is characterized as an event of human discourse that is goaded and elevated by the Word of God.

He proposes the concept of recollection as God's revelation immanent in every human existence, i.e., human's original awareness of God (I/1, 99). The church finds its source of the divine Word only when it returns to its own being of Jesus Christ. And the church steps into its proclamation through the prophetic and apostolic witness. On the interpretation of the Scripture, Barth voices the principle of exegesis in stating, "Thus, exegesis, without which the norm cannot itself as a norm, entails the constant danger that the Bible will be taken prisoner by the church (. . .)" (I/1, 106).

God became the human word, as recorded in the Bible, and thus, God's Word. And this Word refers to its being in the process of becoming, as opposed to our grasping and accepting it with faith. In other words, the becoming is an event where biblical words become God's Word as they come into play with the word of human witness. Human words are bearers of the eternal Word, yet we can never equate the Bible with the revelation itself, i.e., Jesus Christ. Notwithstanding the juxtaposed episodes that exist within the Bible, the unity of revelation guarantees the coherence of the biblical message, even amid conflicting elements. Consequently, Barth categorizes the Word into three distinct classifications:

1. The Word of God (Jesus Christ).
2. The Written Word.
3. The Preached Word.

Thus, the Word of God is disclosed through Revelation, Scripture, and Proclamation.

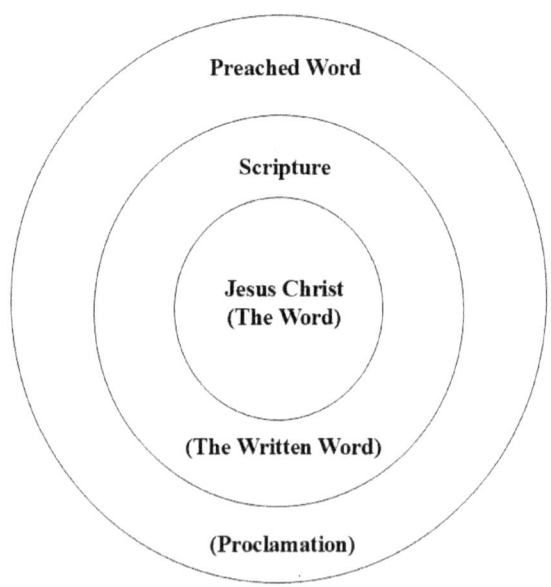

Barth's concept of the threefold form of the Word of God can be observed through what I call a dialectical movement: forward and backward. The forward movement is evident when we read the Scriptures, which testify about Jesus Christ as the embodiment of truth, while the backward movement occurs when we interpret the same Scriptures in the light of Christ. This twofold movement is what I would consider to be one of the most significant contributions of Barth to Christian theology.

5. The Nature of the Word of God

God's Word is God's speech that continuously speaks to us through his acts and mysteries, which are primarily spiritual and only then as a natural or physical event. "God's Word (. . .) It is not "a truth," not even the very highest truth. It is *the* truth (. . .)" (I/1, 136). This truth, which is disclosed through proclamation and Scripture, must be comprehended within the context of Jesus Christ and not anywhere else.

The Father, Son, and Holy Spirit have love as their object, even without the existence of the world or creation. The Triune God could satisfy his love in himself, but his Word has come to us as the Word of reconciliation, i.e., God's Word itself has become God's act. This Word of God, who is Jesus Christ, is above the biblical witness of prophets and apostles. As a result, there is no escape from the power of this Word spoken by God in Jesus Christ. God's Word is the ultimate power to which humans are subject to its claim, regardless of their attitude. Thus, "the Word of God is first understood as decision or it is not understood at all" (I/1, 157). The Word of God is an uncreated reality that is solely identified with God himself (I/1, 158). And the power of God's Word governs a twofold possibility of decision and choice, where God's decision determines what our own decision should be. In sum, human choices find their ground and sustenance in God's decision.

Amid the theological discourse, Barth addresses the issue of pride within the discipline, notably our presumption that we are capable of comprehending it fully. Nevertheless, the Word of God is disclosed through the context of creaturely reality, despite the creature's inherent fallenness. He subsequently shifts the discourse to the concept of secularity, asserting, "But incarnation means entry into this secularity" (I/1, 168). Through this lens of secularity, Barth posits that God veils and unveils himself. But a secular form without the divine content is not the Word of God, and vice versa. Furthermore, he highlights a methodology in which faith arises from hearing God's Word, emphasizing that faith itself is a work of the Holy Spirit. Thus, God's Word is the mystery of the Spirit imprinted on our hearts and lips, over our choices.

6. The Knowability of the Word of God

After establishing the foundation of the reality of the Word of God across its three distinct forms, Barth observes that Jesus Christ embodies the Word of God and the essence of the church, facilitating the sinner's access to a genuine understanding of the Word. Human beings can attain knowledge of God solely through the divine will. This genuine comprehension is rendered possible when the Word is imparted to us by the Holy Spirit (I/1, 199). It is noteworthy that in Barth's theology of the knowability of God, Christology and pneumatology work in tandem to reveal God's knowledge to us.

Barth articulates three fundamental points to substantiate his argument regarding the exclusivity of the Word of God:

1. The Word of God is inherently sufficient and does not require validation from alternative sources.
2. The Word needs no necessity to depend on anthropological principles, which have historically exhibited an inherent skepticism within theological discourse.
3. The potency of the Word of God is adequate to respond to human self-determination, thereby eliminating the requirement to ground it in concealed anthropological constructs.

The power of God's Word does not break humans but bends them into conformity with itself. There is no experience, except for the ambivalence that is deeply rooted in the nature of the Word itself, which is appropriated as a gift of the Holy Spirit, making God's Word God's act upon humans. Thus, human stands as a conjunction or synthesis of the Word, which becomes possible through the process of impartation (I/1, 212).

In acknowledging the impartation, humanity receives the opportunity for experience and knowledge of the Word of God. The essence of the human experience of God's Word is fundamentally rooted in acknowledging God's Word. Barth advances his argument by delineating the promise, on the one hand, as the Word of God encountered in revelation, Scripture, and proclamation, and, on the other hand, by asserting that there is no genuine knowledge of the Word that is devoid of the execution of this act of acknowledgment.

What, then, constitutes acknowledgment? Barth elucidates that the internal dimension of the Christian experience itself serves as a testament to the genuine acknowledgment of the Word of God, which is bestowed upon humanity (I/1, 224). In discussing the authenticity of God's knowability, he posits that the resolution resides in the assurance of grace that has already been received, manifested through the grace of faith and baptism. Hence, "(. . .) the knowledge of God's Word is no other than the reality of the grace of God coming to man (. . .)" (I/1, 227). This event of grace cannot be worked out or produced by us, except by letting it speak for itself. Thus, the Word of God is given as the object of acknowledgment and, therefore, the real basis for faith that needs ongoing contemplation.

Barth examines the theme of faith and asserts that God grants humans the capacity to possess faith, as the essence of faith is bestowed upon humanity (I/1, 238). Through faith, individuals are enabled to attain the alignment and ability necessary to receive God's Word. This reception is facilitated through the proclamation of faith and the confession of the Word. According to Barth, faith is imparted to humanity through the Word, which individuals experience and respond to. Ultimately, he emphasizes that the potential to comprehend the Word of God represents a divine miracle. Christ does not remain outside, knocking at the door, as referenced in Rev. 3:20; instead, he traverses through closed doors, as conveyed in John 20:19 (I/1, 247).

7. The Word of God, Dogma, and Dogmatics

Barth recounts that the Word of God exists in three distinct forms: revealed, written, and preached. He contends that the Word of God is inherently incomprehensible to humanity. Consequently, the undertaking of dogmatics is to evaluate whether the declarations made by the church are consistent with the Word of God or not (I/1, 250). Furthermore, theology functions as the standard for evaluating the church's declarations and their implementation in alignment with God's Word.

He further asserts four fundamental criteria in examining the relationship between the Word and the church's proclamation:

1. The Word of God must serve as the standard for the church's proclamation.
2. The church's proclamation must derive its content exclusively from God's Word.
3. Barth asserts, "It is in force before and as proclamation is undertaken; proclamation is undertaken on the basis of the fact that it is already in force" (I/1, 256).
4. Other disciplines cannot serve as criteria alongside or independent of the Word of God.

Consequently, he articulates the dual function of the church, wherein it, on one hand, proclaims the Word of God and, on the other hand, must allow itself to be consistently corrected, critiqued, and governed by the same Word of God.

He advances his argument by saying that the church embodies the teachings of Jesus Christ, provided that the Word of God persists as the speech, the act, and the mystery. In other words, the

Word of God is perceived as a mystery revealed through human language. Consequently, the objective of dogmatics is to engage with the Word of God (Holy Scripture) alongside the Word of humanity (Church proclamation) to the extent that both serve as witnesses to the third and original form of revelation, namely, Jesus Christ (I/1, 265). Indeed, Jesus Christ serves as the only revelation, from which the Scriptures and proclamations derive their purpose and sustenance.

In the context of Roman Catholic theology, Barth argues that dogmatics should strive for the truth of revelation rather than merely engaging in an investigation. This distinction arises from the fact that dogma targets the truth of revelation, while dogmatics endeavors to ascertain the same through propositional statements. Subsequently, the church is unable to prescribe commands to the dogmas, as it possesses the truth of doctrine. Instead, the Word of God is communicated to the church, which is comprised of assembled sinners, as the Word of the Lord.

"Dogma," Barth writes, "is the relation between the God who commands and the man who obeys His command (. . .)" (I/1, 274). Here, he makes an interesting distinction between regular and irregular dogmatics. Regular or academic dogmatics encompass all the significant themes of Church proclamation, while irregular dogmatics proceed without any primary task in mind, instead presenting free discussions of the issues that arise in church proclamation (I/1, 277). He also notes that regular dogmatics are healthier for Protestantism today, while pointing out the risk that irregular dogmatics may be influenced by the personal experiences and biographies of their authors. "What finally counts is whether a dogmatics is scriptural" or not (I/1, 287).

He concludes the chapter by examining the epistemology of dogmatics. The primary objective of the path of knowledge in dogmatics is to recognize that in Holy Scripture and church dogmatics, one engages with the Word of God (Jesus Christ). And God's Word represents God's speech, act, and mystery.

Chapter 2

The Revelation of God

PART 1: THE TRIUNE GOD

8. God in His Revelation

Barth articulates, "God's Word is God Himself in His revelation" (I/1, 295). He proposes to initiate the inquiry with the doctrine of the Trinity in order to arrive at the doctrine of revelation. He argues that the doctrine of the Trinity must be positioned as the foremost element of all other dogmatics, as it distinctly differentiates the Christian doctrines from all other doctrines and concepts (I/1, 301). In this revelation of God's freedom, God identifies himself as "I" and addresses us as "Thou" (I/1, 307). This profound relationship serves as the foundation of revelation, which is intrinsic to the doctrine of the Trinity as attested in the Holy Scripture.

In Revelation, God "makes Himself the object of human contemplation, human experience, human thought, and human speech" (I/1, 315). God presents himself dialectically by concealing and manifesting or by veiling and unveiling. This dialectical address of God can be observed when God differentiated himself from himself as the second mode, the Son. But, the act of revelation "(. . .) does not mean in the slightest a loss of His mystery" (I/1, 324). In other words, God's revelation remains intact and unimpaired throughout its interaction with humanity. The nature of this revelation is a record of events that have occurred once and for all in a specific time and place.

In conclusion, Barth critically examines *vestigium trinitatis* by interrogating the feasibility of revelation existing independently through forms, concepts, and ideas. In response, he argues that humanity, in its quest to articulate the mystery of God, formulated this dogma using biblical and philosophical terminology. Regrettably, this endeavor has led to a misrepresentation of the original intention to convey revelation, resulting in a discourse that counters God's revelation; "The conqueror was conquered" (I/1, 344). He further notices the danger of any attempt to leave the words of Scripture; we have already departed from revelation to a dangerous possibility with our mouths and pens (I/1, 345). Thus, revelation can only be derived from Scripture and not from human consciousness. And we can only point to the root of revelation to the doctrine of the Trinity. The *vestigium creaturae in trinitate* is reliable, and we ought to adhere only to the root of the doctrine of the Trinity. In sum, the Scripture finds its ground in the revelation of Jesus Christ, which in turn finds its roots in the Trinity (Scripture—Revelation (Jesus Christ)—Trinity).

9. The Triunity of God

According to Barth, the doctrine of the Trinity emphasizes a singular being with a single name, who is the sole "Willer" and "Doer." Nevertheless, the Trinitarian baptismal formula, often misunderstood as three divine names, is contrary to this belief. In contrast, Barth contends that the triadic reference to the Father, Son, and Holy Spirit is firmly rooted in the Godhead, wherein each iteration signifies the one and the same God. He acknowledges the peril posed by the church's confusing tritheism with monotheism, to which the church must resolutely respond with a definitive 'No.'

We notice that Barth's exploration of the Trinity is centered around two fundamental questions. Firstly, what does it mean to assert that there is the same being in Father, Son, and the Holy

Spirit? Secondly, what is the definition of the term "person"? "Therefore, by preference," Barth states, "we do not use the term 'person' but rather 'mode' (. . .) the same thing as is meant by 'person'" (I/1, 359). He answers them, by identifying that God brings himself to humanity in two ways: on one hand, we see Father, Son, and the Holy Spirit as pointing to the knowledge and concept of one God, and on the other hand, the source and goal of this trinity is never one but three (I/1, 369).

In addition, the Father can be perceived as the ultimate "Giver," the Son as both the "Receiver and Giver," and the Spirit as the "pure Receiver," thereby positing the doctrine of the Trinity as a self-contained circle that points to God as the sole revealer. Nevertheless, the biblical witness does not explicitly declare that these three figures possess equal essence, nor does it denote them as three distinct modes of being of God. Indeed, the dual aspect of the Trinity extends beyond the parameters of biblical testimony (I/1, 381).

10. God the Father

Barth proceeds with his discourse on the doctrine of the Trinity by concentrating on the person of the Father. He underscores that God engages with humanity with definitive superiority through Jesus of Nazareth. "And it should be clear," Barth states, "(. . .) as the Father of Jesus Christ, that God is called our creator" (I/1, 389). In other words, the unknown Father is revealed to us in Jesus, who shows us the creator as our Father.

However, Barth articulates a critical argument positing that the Son derives his essence from the Father, while the Spirit originates from the Father; the Father is recognized as the singular source of the Trinity. The Father, Son, and Holy Spirit share in the same essence as the Father, yet each does not represent a second or third aspect of God (I/1, 394). Consequently, this directs us toward an understanding of the Trinity aligned with the doctrine of perichoresis. We see Barth wrestling with the dialectical view of Father being, in some sense, the originator, yet he upholds that the Son and the Spirit are no less than the Father.

11. God the Son

Barth begins this section by presenting a preliminary to the upcoming base rule for the Father-Son relationship as an eternal one.

> What God reveals in Jesus and how he reveals it, namely, in Jesus, must not be separated from one another (. . .) seriously we have to regard the concept of God as the Father in his relation to this mediator of his revelation as a mode of being which truly and definitely appertains to him; we have to regard this Fatherhood as an eternal one (I/1, 399).

Barth firmly believes that the relationship between the Father and the Son is eternal rather than temporal or functional. He believes that Jesus is a complete and true God, without any reduction or limitation. He suggests that when speaking about creation, we must use the first mode (Father) of being, and when talking about reconciliation, we must use the second mode (Son) of being. Therefore, Barth argues that the Father and Son are in an irreversible relationship, asserting that "(. . .) God is God the Son and He is God the Father. Jesus Christ, the Son of God, is God Himself as God his Father is God Himself" (I/1, 414).

Barth regards the second article of the Nicaeno-Constantinopolitan Creed as having significant importance concerning the deity of Christ, as he examines it with considerable enthusiasm. He articulates that the term "begotten" underscores the oneness, exclusivity, and uniqueness of Christ. Furthermore, he elucidates, "(. . .) He is antecedently in Himself light of light, very God of very God, the begotten of God and not His creature" (I/1, 428).

He employs an analogy of the sun and sunlight to elucidate this relationship more effectively. Just as sunlight is emanated and derived from the sun, so too does Jesus Christ originate from the Father. The relation between the Father and the Son transcends mere symbolism, established as the original and appropriate non-symbolic essence inherent in that creaturely reality. "The eternal Word," Barth asserts, "concealed in God, Jesus Christ Himself" (I/1, 436). Consequently, both creation and revelation constitute a singular reality of Jesus Christ in conjunction with the Father, and serve as both the creator and the revealer.

12. God the Holy Spirit

Barth initiates his discourse on the Holy Spirit by posing a pertinent question: How do individuals come to recognize that Jesus is Lord? In addressing this inquiry, he answers that the Spirit of God forges the relationship between God and the existence of the creature. The Holy Spirit does not constitute an independent entity; instead, it serves as an illumination, stimulation, and instruction through the Word and for the Word, i.e., Jesus Christ (I/1, 453).

He examines the work of the Holy Spirit in three principal points. Firstly, the Holy Spirit affirms and validates the Word of God through divine revelation, i.e., all faith, knowledge, and obedience possessed by humanity originate from the Holy Spirit. Secondly, the Holy Spirit guides individuals in ways they cannot accomplish independently. Lastly, the Holy Spirit equips individuals with the means to articulate the message of Christ and realize a new existence by affirming that the Holy Spirit is both God himself and not distinct from him.

Towards the conclusion of the first part of volume one, Barth discusses a pivotal argument regarding the human condition by stating, "Even in receiving the Holy Ghost, man remains man, the sinner sinner" (I/1, 462). He then sets the base rule "(. . .) that statements about the divine modes of being antecedently in themselves cannot be different in content from those that are (. . .) in revelation (. . .) what is called the immanent Trinity" are "the indispensable premises of the economic Trinity" (I/1, 479). His base rule can be perceived as an anticipated risk associated with relinquishing human presuppositions that may conflict with the revelation of God in Jesus Christ. Hence, the Father and Son are united in the communion of the Spirit through love, and this union of love defines God and facilitates the expression of God's love towards creation.

The Doctrine of the Word of God
(Vol. I/2)

Chapter 2

The Revelation of God

PART 2: THE INCARNATION OF THE WORD

13. God's Freedom for Humans

Barth commences part two of volume one with a persistent affirmation that the revelation found within the holy Scriptures originates from the Father and is objectively actualized in the Son while subjectively realized through the work of the Holy Spirit.[1] Revelation can be seen as a reciprocal relationship between God and humanity, asserting that the knowledge of God in revelation is attainable due to God's will and actions exercised in his freedom. Our appropriate response to revelation involves aligning ourselves to the revelation that serves as the answer (I/2, 26).

Having established the objectivity of revelation in Jesus Christ, Barth advances his argument by posing a critical inquiry regarding the extent to which we can comprehend the revelation manifested in the reality of Jesus Christ. He responds by proposing that it is necessary to understand the existence of Jesus Christ as the objective possibility of revelation, which embodies God's freedom. In essence, God's revelation corresponds directly to the reality of Jesus Christ. "Revelation itself," Barth asserts, "is needed

1. Barth, *Church Dogmatics* I/2, 1; hereafter cited as I/2.

for knowing that God is hidden and man blind. Revelation (. . .) separates God and human by bringing them together" (I/2, 29). This presents a dialectical identity where, in revelation, we are united with God while simultaneously maintaining our distinction from him.

God, in his full divinity, became a human being. Even before the world existed, God was always ready and open to us with his Word or Son (I/2, 34). The Word, by becoming flesh, entered the hiddenness in "servant-form" (*kenosis*), from the "divine form." "By becoming flesh," Barth states, "the Word is no less true and entire God than He was previously in eternity in Himself" (I/2, 38). In order for God to reveal himself, an incarnation was deemed necessary. Thus, through the manifestation of the Word in flesh, the objective possibility of God's revelation was established.

14. The Time of Revelation

The presence of Jesus Christ is an event that represents God's time for us. "If God's revelation has a time," Barth writes, "(. . .) it must be a different time, created alongside of our time and the time originally created by God" (I/2, 47). In other words, when the Word was incarnated, it also assumed the nature of time, which is characterized as God's own time that is inherently self-driven, autonomous, and self-sufficient. It embodies the complete past, present, and future, as it is wholly revealed to us.

In elucidating the divine actions throughout time, he elaborates on the relation between the Old and New Testaments, highlighting three significant aspects:

1. The Old Testament, akin to the New Testament, serves as a testimony to revelation, which is a definitive and singular act of God.
2. The Old Testament bears witness to the revelation in which God remains and asserts his identity as the hidden God.

3. The Old Testament, like the New Testament, is a witness to the revelation of God present to humans as the forthcoming God (I/2, 94).

Thus, the messianic hope of Israel alludes to an authentic historical occurrence.

Now, Barth shifts to the passion narratives and the resurrection of Christ, positing that God himself enters into the darkness so that sinful humanity remains unscathed by the profound bitterness of his wrath or death (I/2, 108). As a result, we are challenged to bear our crosses and follow Christ. And the resurrection is presented as the event that reveals the incarnate, the humiliated, and the crucified Christ, wherein the prophets and apostles were not witnesses to the resurrection itself; instead, the resurrection encapsulated them. In conclusion, the bodily resurrection can be understood as a significant culmination of Christian witness, rather than merely a symbol, ultimately indicating the prospect of human resurrection (I/2, 117).

15. The Mystery of Revelation

In the exploration of the enigmatic nature of revelation as reconciliation, a notable indicator of the resurrection of Jesus Christ is the miracle of his birth, which was conceived through the Holy Spirit and brought forth by the Virgin Mary. The eternal Word embodies the mystery of revelation and directs attention to Jesus Christ as the foundational beginning of our understanding (I/2, 124). The Word maintained its essence throughout the process of becoming flesh; however, it manifested as a genuine human entity, serving as a medium in the demonstration of divine acts, thereby constituting both a revelation and a miracle. As Barth articulates, "In so doing, he did not cease to be what he was before, but became what he was not before, a man" (I/2, 149), thereby rendering the eternal Word accessible to humanity.

Barth perceives the revelation of God in Christ as humanity acknowledging its state of lostness and existing entirely by virtue of God's mercy. This merciful act of revelation and reconciliation ought to be recognized as being inherent in the Christmas message. God has concealed himself within humanity through Christmas, thereby revealing himself in the empty tomb. "The Virgin birth," Barth states, "denotes particularly the mystery of revelation" (I/2, 182). He interprets the fundamental significance of the Virgin birth as indicative of a precise limitation while also imparting grace to it. Furthermore, he investigates the Virgin birth not as a disavowal of sinful sexual life, but rather as a symbol denoting the exclusion of sinful sexual life as its origin (I/2, 191).

The virginity of Mary symbolizes the profound revelation and mystery associated with Christmas. The reference to the Holy Spirit in the context of the virgin birth can be understood in two interpretations: first, the human existence of Jesus Christ is a mystery that originates from God himself; second, the role of the Holy Spirit serves as a vital link between our reconciliation and the essence of the reconciler (I/2, 199). Jesus Christ was conceived through the Holy Spirit and born of the Virgin Mary; he embodies both the conceived and the born. Therefore, the miracle of the virgin birth is founded upon the mystery, and this miracle serves as a testament to that mystery.

PART 3: THE OUTPOURING OF THE HOLY SPIRIT

16. The Freedom of Humans for God

In this section, Barth posits that the inquiry regarding God's self-revelation can only be conducted within the framework of the revelation attested within the Bible. He examines the notion of God as the Revealer, the act of revelation, and the concept of revealedness. He underscores that the subjective reality of revelation emerges from the outpouring of the Holy Spirit, which constitutes not a human action in revelation but rather God's action for and upon humanity (I/2, 205).

He notes that the church is the place where God transforms humans into recipients of his revelation, and it has no independent reality apart from Jesus Christ. He identifies the church's origin in Jesus Christ in four ways. Firstly, the church derives its subjective reality of revelation from Jesus Christ. Secondly, it is composed of the children of God who are born and will die for the omnipotent Word of grace. Thirdly, the church primarily embodies the life of a community that relies on the incarnate Word. And fourthly, the subjective reality of revelation is divine-human, eternal-temporal, and visible-invisible (I/2, 219). Thus, the relation between the Word and the church is mediated subjectively and objectively through the outpouring of the Holy Spirit.

Barth further says that revelation constitutes a divine act of condescension toward humanity, wherein humans do not serve as co-workers but are instead mere recipients of divine revelation (I/2, 237). And the Holy Spirit is identified as the subjective reality of this revelation, which serves to reiterate and affirm the objective revelation bestowed upon us. In other words, the subjective aspect of revelation is intrinsically bound within its objective counterpart. Barth observes the interplay between the Word and the Holy Spirit, stating, "(. . .) the Word is never apart from the Holy Spirit" (I/2, 244), who presents God directly to our hearts and minds, effectively rendering the reality of God's actions.

On a concluding note, Barth comprehends God's revealedness as God himself in person and work through the outpouring of the Holy Spirit. As a result, in the possibility of revelation, we are always on the decreasing end, and God is on the increasing end (I/2, 279).

17. The Revelation of God as the Abolition of Religion

The event of revelation cannot be perceived merely as an interaction between God and humanity; instead, it is an event that uniquely engages human beings in response to God's command. As Barth argues, "Revelation is God's sovereign action upon man, or it is not" (I/2, 295). The notion of revelation is invalidated when it is construed as merely a dialogue, rendering human endeavors to comprehend God ineffective. In addition, he posits that revelation and religion may be conceptualized as identical manifestations of the event involving God and humanity, wherein God assumes the role of Lord and Master over humanity. And the church, through the medium of grace, emerges as the true embodiment of true religion (I/2, 298). As he nails that "(. . .) it is only through truth that truth can come to man" (I/2, 302). The religion is never the truth, but a complete fiction because a religion dies with the rise of another religion, making the revelation of God deny any so-called true religion. Nevertheless, in the context of revelation, individuals who possess vacuous hearts and empty hands are wholly reliant upon the divine revelation. Thus, he places religion as subordinate to revelation.

The revelation is mediated only through grace by which God reveals himself to humans. In other words, the revelation of God is mediated only through grace, and no religion can stand before it as a true religion; contrary to the Christian religion, which is effective through proclamation in its revelation (I/2, 327). Self-awareness of the Christian religion is a gift of grace amid our weakness. Well then, how do humans respond to grace? Barth answers that any human resistance to grace is overshadowed by the overwhelming power of grace itself; "(. . .) grace of God that infinitely contradicts this contradiction" (I/2, 338). In other words, the grace of God is the negation of negation. The creation and election of the Christian religion as the true religion is confirmed only through the grace of Jesus Christ.

18. The Life of the Children of God

Barth acknowledges the testimony of the Holy Scriptures in three ways:

1. Through the unity of Father, Son, and Holy Spirit in God.
2. Through the incarnation of Jesus Christ.
3. Through the outpouring of the Holy Spirit.

For Barth, the essence of Christian living begins and ends with love. "God is love," Barth writes, "before He loves us and apart from it" (I/2, 379). He has demonstrated profound love for us even before we attained the capacity to reciprocate such affection, to the extent that nothing further could be attained by us. Similarly, God also presents himself as the bearer of our shame and curse.

In his exploration of God's love, Barth identifies that our love for God takes place in the self-knowledge of repentance, in which we learn about ourselves by the mirror of the Word of God. "It is grace," Barth asserts, "that God wills not only to love us but to be loved by us in return" (I/2, 395). And our love, in return, finds its necessary love for the neighbor as the responsibility bestowed by the creator. In other words, when surrounded by love for God, we are captivated by the greater circle of love that includes love for our neighbor as a necessity. Helping our neighbor remove her sufferings is the object of our proper worship of God, as Jesus Christ is always concealed in the neighbor. Here, Barth takes the side of Calvin over Luther in acknowledging that in our relationship with our neighbor, the road does not lead from Law to Gospel but from Gospel to Law (I/2, 437). Thus, we can appropriately express our love for our neighbor solely by engaging in prayer for ourselves and reflecting on the fulfilled promises stemming from the work of Jesus Christ (I/2, 454).

Chapter 3

Holy Scripture

19. The Word of God for the church

Barth transitions to the doctrine of holy Scripture, positing that, on the one hand, it serves as a witness to divine revelation, the Word of God, through the Holy Spirit. On the other hand, holy Scripture reflects the appropriate attitude of obedience toward this witness. This implies that all church declarations and our testimonies need to be rooted in obedience to Scripture. The witness of holy Scripture, through the unity of the Old and New Testaments, confirms it as the divine revelation, as the very Word of God. It is not a divine impartation but a genuine witness (I/2, 507). This scriptural witness requires proclamation through preaching and the administration of the sacraments to be the Word of God. He asserts that we have only one Word of God, the eternal Word of the Father that became flesh, and the holy Scriptures are his witnesses to this Word and its presence (I/2, 513). In other words, the Scriptures become the Word of God, rather than being the Word of God. It is noteworthy that in Barth's theology, the Scriptures are understood as a process or an event. These assertions by Barth undoubtedly establish Jesus Christ as the preeminent Word in relation to Scripture and the church's proclamation.

In furthering the discourse, Barth identifies the Scriptures as "a genuine fallible human word is at this centre the Word of God" (I/2, 530). However, God takes this human word and uses it like the water in the pool of Bethesda. Barth argued that God is not ashamed of the fallibility of human words and their historical and scientific inaccuracies. Instead, God adopts and uses this fallible witness, which is known as verbal inspiration (I/2, 533). On the contrary, he cautions that it is our disobedience if we try to find infallible elements in the Bible. Nevertheless, the Scripture ought to be recognized as the Word of God through the mediating work of the Holy Spirit.

20. Authority in the Church

Barth posits that the influence of sacred Scriptures is manifested through the mediating presence of the Holy Spirit in the revelation of Jesus Christ. He insists the church should go beyond the representative, i.e., Scripture, to the supreme judge and Lord (I/2, 541). The church cannot disregard the importance of Scripture. Instead, it should recognize that the Scriptures bear witness to the incarnation of the Word of God and the outpouring of the Holy Spirit, which are essential in every age for the church's authentic witness. For Barth, the church should look up to Christ, the Holy Spirit, and the Father as its divine glory and authority. "In the church," Barth writes, "(. . .) obedience towards Jesus Christ and subjection to His authority are not an open question (. . .)" (I/2, 580). However, it is a command to be embraced and followed. "Under the Word, which means Holy Scripture, the church must and can live, whereas beyond or beside the Word it can only die" (I/2, 585). Consequently, the existence and sustenance of the church are fundamentally rooted in its relationship with Christ and the Spirit, as conveyed through the Scriptures.

He further examines the authority of the church and affirms it as genuinely established in the common hearing and receiving of the Word of God. In addition, the church's authority is based on its confession and exists in faith and obedience to the Word of God

(I/2, 596). On the same lines, a person's authority in the church is determined by their interpretation of the Word of God in their service to it.

The nature of the church's calling is universal and rooted in the holy Scriptures (I/2, 622). And all confessions of the church must consist of freedom, joyous responsibility, and love that ought to be evaluated in the light of the holy Scripture. "The church's confession," Barth states, "(. . .) to be read as a first commentary on the Holy Scripture" (I/2, 649). But this confession can never equate to the revelation and the church, as it violates the divine authority of holy Scripture. Thus, all the confessions of the church are relative and not absolute, except that the church as the body is eternally united to its Lord.

21. Freedom in the Church

Barth notices an inseparable unity between authority and freedom in the holy Scriptures under the Word of God. He indeed understands them as predicates of God's Word, and only in the light of this Word, i.e., Jesus Christ, are they cast upon each other (I/2, 666). This freedom within the church also constitutes a human freedom that can never exist independently of, nor contradict, the Word; instead, it remains subordinate to the Word. Similarly, the prophets and apostles of their time chose to live in obedience to Jesus Christ, for "(. . .) even obedience is freedom" (I/2, 670).

"A freedom under the Word," Barth asserts, "is not a secure possession (. . .) but a gift from divine mercy, continually to be received as such, and only as such" (I/2, 697). This freedom in the church is exercised through its interpretation and its responsibility towards the holy Scripture. To interpret the holy Scripture, we need to subordinate ourselves to the word of the prophets and apostles (Scripture) in love and fear. It is noteworthy that Barth positions Jesus Christ as the ultimate Word, and only in the light of Christ should holy Scriptures be understood and interpreted. Hence, we need to subordinate our ideas, thoughts, and convictions to the witness of the prophets and apostles that confront us in Scripture (I/2, 718).

Chapter 4

The Proclamation of the Church

22. The Mission of the Church

The proclamation of the church is a human word spoken in confirmation of the biblical witness, which creates obedience to the Word of God. This Word becomes a law and a duty for those in the church. "Jesus Christ," Barth affirms, "in the power of His resurrection is present wherever men really speak really of God" (I/2, 752). So, humans are called to the preaching ministry through which God performs and operates through grace and miracles.

In exploring the ministry of preaching, he posits that it is not just a human effort but a self-proclamation of the Word of God. He elaborates this by using the concepts of theory and doctrine. Theory is the human observation and thinking that can describe and interpret things, and doctrine is the impartation of something taught using proper communication and received with proper understanding (I/2, 761). The doctrine alone cannot bring Jesus Christ or establish a fellowship between God and human unless it is in the work of pure grace.

He further identifies three interdependent tasks of dogmatics. Firstly, biblical theology deals with the question of its foundation. Secondly, practical theology addresses the question of its form. Thirdly, dogmatic theology focuses on the content of Church preaching and how it aligns with the revelation stated in Scripture (I/2, 766). Pure doctrine is a promise given to the church as a result of the grace of the Word of God and the obedience of faith that arises from it. So, Barth identifies dogmatics and preaching as inseparable duties of the church. "Certainly," Barth writes, "dogmatics cannot ask concerning the absolute purity of doctrine—for it is not the work of man, but of God to produce this" (I/2, 777).

Barth subtly shifts his gears in investigating the relationship between dogmatics and ethics. He proposes that the Word of God cannot be considered merely a historical medium; instead, it needs to be viewed in the context of theological ethics. "Dogmatics has no option," Barth asserts, "it has to be ethics as well" (I/2, 793). And, the task of integrating ethics into dogmatics can be accomplished by recognizing the following conditions:

1. The separation of dogmatics and ethics can only be technical and not based on principles.
2. Dogmatics should be closely related to ethical problems.
3. Ethics must be subordinate to dogmatics. The mutual interaction between dogmatics and ethics can be observed, with dogmatics offering marginal control over ethics.

23. Dogmatics as a Function of the Hearing Church

Barth argues that the essential truth of dogmatics in the church proclamation lies in God speaking for himself through the human word. The human word in the church proclamation is both the beginning and end of dogmatics. "Dogmatics is, therefore, a call to order and unity in the church" (I/2, 802). And the redemption of the church proclamation lies in teaching Jesus Christ and eventually transitioning from teaching to hearing him in the promise of the Word, which became flesh.

He furthers the discourse on dogmatics by reminding the teaching Church to listen to Jesus Christ's voice. "The dogmatician can only place himself alongside the preacher and not over him" (I/2, 813). In other words, both dogmatics and dogmaticians should subordinate themselves to the witness to Jesus Christ, holy Scripture and preaching, and strive towards an ecumenical church dogmatics.

Similarly, he also argues, "The church dogmatics is Evangelical dogmatics, or it is not Church dogmatics" (I/2, 825). He then defines Evangelical dogmatics as a one, holy, universal, apostolic church that is purified and founded anew by the reformers, driven by the Word of God as the only possible normative determination. In other words, the Evangelical Church is the church of Jesus Christ that separates itself from the three heresies, Neo-Protestantism, Roman Catholicism, and Eastern Orthodoxy by establishing its church dogmatics as necessarily reformed dogmatics. It is significant to note that Barth, on one hand, endeavors to establish an ecumenical church, and on the other hand, he positions the Evangelical church as the epitome of the universal church. However, as we remain an Evangelical Church, he proposes that we must also be open to others' common faith and authority in the holy Scriptures, and receive correction when recommended. Dogmatics for Barth are "(. . .) purified and reconstituted by the work of Calvin and the confession which sealed his testimony" (I/2, 831). It is evident that Barth illuminates Calvin and his contributions to a greater extent than those of other reformers.

The Word of God can only be found in the church, and not in an academy. "If, therefore, an academy is required to serve the Word of God, it can only be the academy of the church, founded and maintained (. . .) by the existence of the Word of God" (I/2, 841). And the church's testimony is to let people hear from the church and, therefore, from dogmatics. Notably, Barth is not in favour of an exclusive academic study of holy Scripture that is independent of the Word and in its relationship with the church.

24. Dogmatics as a Function of the Teaching Church

Barth begins the final section of volume one by stating that "the one Church is both the hearing and the teaching Church. It can never be the one without the other" (I/2, 844). He lays out a clear distinction between the dogmatician and the dogmatic method. Where the dogmatician, in essence, lives in obedience to say what she has heard and to give what she has received, and the dogmatic method consists of the work carried out in love, fear, and reverence in presenting the contents of the Word of God, rather than the human subject. "Therefore," Barth states, "dogmatics must actually be Christology and only Christology" (I/2, 872).

In conclusion, he comprehends the contents of dogmatics in its address to four main topics:

1. The doctrine of God.
2. The doctrine of creation.
3. The doctrine of atonement.
4. The doctrine of redemption.

In all our pursuits, Barth upholds that one should uphold God alone, who uses humans to proclaim his thoughts and speak his word.

The Doctrine of God (Vol. II/1)

Chapter 5

The Knowledge of God

25. The Fulfillment of the Knowledge of God

Barth commences volume two by establishing that in the church of Jesus Christ, humans speak about God and must hear about God. "But only that which is fulfilled under the constraint of God's Word is such a true knowledge of God."[1] And any other knowledge or approach besides Jesus Christ can lead us to false gods. Real knowledge of God lies in God's relationship with humanity, while he still remains distinct from humans. In the knowledge of God, we observe, on the one hand, God setting himself as our object, and on the other hand, positioning us as knowers of him through grace. We receive truth only in the form of grace by the active will of God. "Thus, the knowledge of God can be understood as the bestowal and reception of this free grace of God" (II/1, 29).

He further suggests that God encounters humans in such a way that, in this encounter, God remains God but elevates humans to know him. He elucidates this in a threefold process: Firstly, God is our love, so when we love him. Secondly, God offers himself as the reason and cause to love him. Finally, God creates the possibility, the willingness, and the readiness to know him. "God stands before man as the One whom he may love and must fear-may

1. Barth, *Church Dogmatics* II/1, 7; hereafter cited as II/1.

really love and must really fear-above all things" (II/1, 35). Here, Barth corrects Luther's order (*Smaller Catechism*) of fear and love to the reverse. We first love God, and in this love, we fear losing this loving God. In addition, God stands before us in clarity and certainty, yet in mystery. This dialectical view of God's knowledge affirms that God is known to us, and in this knowing, he still remains hidden from us.

In exploring the idea of human elevation, he suggests that God elevates us to himself through his speech while humbling himself to us. The reality of knowing God lies in the reciprocal relationship between God and the objects (humans) he created (II/1, 58). This relationship is often referred to as the "Thou and He" relationship. Therefore, God's self-knowledge consists in the participation that runs continually and sacramentally, through the self-witness of God.

26. The Knowability of God

Barth establishes the fact that the readiness of God is the first instance of the knowability of God. "This knowledge of God," Barth writes, "is wholly and utterly His own readiness to be known by us, grounded in His being and activity" (II/1, 66). And this knowledge is possible because God is knowable to himself at first. In this self-awareness of God, we see a "divine encroachment" through which God is rendered and made possible to us in grace (II/1, 69).

What is grace? "Grace is God's good-pleasure" (II/1, 74). And Jesus Christ is the reality of God's good pleasure. It is in our relationship with Jesus Christ that God's knowability has taken place prior to our decisions. "It is not even partly because of this previous knowledge and partly because of God's revelation. It is in the consequence of God's revelation alone" (II/1, 76). Therefore, all human decisions ultimately point to God's decision in Christ, to which we respond with gratitude.

In this context, Barth quickly detours into natural theology, countering that it cannot even be discussed as a principle within the church. He proposes that natural theology is an idol that contradicts the holy Scriptures. God's knowability is impossible in any revelation apart from God's revelation, which was mediated only through grace and mercy.

In moving to the discourse on the readiness of humans, Barth affirms, "(. . .) the readiness of God is God's grace. Hence, the readiness of man must obviously be his readiness for grace" (II/1, 129). Unfortunately, humans are not at peace but at war and enmity with grace. But this enmity is conquered only by Jesus Christ, who is our readiness and the grace of God. Thus, "the readiness of man included in the readiness of God is Jesus Christ. And therefore, Jesus Christ is the knowability of God on our side (. . .) the knowability of God on God's side" (II/1, 150). Christ indeed is the mediating grace that bridges helpless humanity into the bosom of the gracious God.

And the readiness of God through Jesus Christ is the triumph of grace over human hostility with grace. Jesus is the eternal representation of the scope of God's knowledge; in him, we stand inside God and not outside. "The fact that by the Holy Spirit," Barth says, "we are ready for God in Jesus Christ (. . .)" (II/1, 157). Thus, humans possess no autonomy apart from Jesus Christ, who has embraced human affirmations as his own.

27. The Limits of the Knowledge of God

Barth begins this paragraph by raising two questions: how much of God is known? And how much is God knowable? He then answers, "(. . .) that God is known by God and by God alone" (II/1, 179). Human beings lack the capacity to engage in fellowship with God due to the hiddenness that exists between God and humanity. "The hiddenness of God is the content of a statement of faith" (II/1, 183). It is through faith and by the divine goodwill that we perceive his hiddenness. And this hiddenness eludes our ability to view, conceive, and articulate, resting solely within the power of God. Nonetheless, we cannot fully grasp God through human endeavors; instead, we are permitted to perceive him in faith, recognizing that this concealed God has been revealed and made known to us exclusively in Jesus Christ. Through the divine gift and authorization, we realize that in Jesus Christ, God's hiddenness is revealed, and we respond in faith through human words. However, these human appropriations must be a perpetual endeavor that needs consistent evaluation.

He further articulates that the veracity of human knowledge finds its foundation in the veracity of divine knowledge. He equates that "the veracity of our knowledge of God is the veracity of His revelation" (II/1, 209). God's revelation is trustworthy as it originates from the Trinitarian God. Our words about God and his revelation are inadequate; however, only through "divine indwelling" do we participate in the truthfulness of the divine revelation. The human conception of God's revelation is legitimized by grace as we communicate in obedience. The hiddenness of God's revelation "(. . .) veils Himself in His revelation, He also unveils Himself" (II/1, 215). It is through this dialectical process of veiling and unveiling that God's revelation has been presented and made accessible to humanity. Consequently, humanity is elevated to comprehend God and articulate thoughts about him with gratitude, thereby transforming the human word into God's word.

Chapter 6

The Reality of God

28. The Being of God as the One Who Loves in Freedom

Barth believes that God expresses his love by seeking fellowship with us. God's love originates in the trinitarian life as Father, Son, and the Holy Spirit. "God is, who He is in His works" (II/1, 260). In other words, God's being is no different from his works. These works constitute revelation as events in history that, on the one hand, were passed by and, on the other hand, are yet to happen. That is to say that "God's being is life," who is constantly engaged in relation with the creation. His being is the only self-moved and self-motivated being, an event of God's very act (II/1, 272). Since we cannot inquire about God's being in eternity, we seek his being in his act, i.e., revelation. Thus, the being of God can be inquired into only from the point of his revelation and not elsewhere.

    God is complete without us, but he chose to love and let his love overflow to us in communion. He has revealed himself to us in absolute love through the person of Jesus Christ. On the one hand, God is free to live and love in revelation, but on the other hand, he is free in himself, apart from his relationship with others. In other words, God is neither bound nor controlled by the creation or revelation. And the extent of God's freedom to reveal himself lies in God alone. "The freedom of God," Barth writes, "is understood primarily as His own positive freedom, it can and must be understood secondarily in His relationship to that which is other than Himself (...)" (II/1, 309). Here, Barth expands the theology of God's being by understanding that, in essence, God is relational and continues to be relational even without humanity. God's essence suffers no loss in the absence of humanity or creation. He is free to be who he is in himself and also free to act contrary to his nature. He embraces the relationship with his creation, yet he remains detached in mystery. And this freedom of God to love us is fulfilled and exercised only in Jesus Christ (II/1, 321).

29. The Perfections of God

Barth establishes God as the perfect being and the standard of all perfection ("attributes"). "There is no possibility," Barth states, "of knowing the perfect God without knowing His perfections" (II/1, 322). We can speak of his perfections only from the ground of his revelation. And it is on this ground that God has authorized human words to proclaim his revelation. "We have thus to recognize" God "both in hiddenness and in His self-disclosure" (II/1, 342). Indeed, the love of God elevates human ideas and concepts to denote God and his perfections through grace. Thus, God's being and perfections are his essence, through which he loves us as he loves himself.

30. The Perfections of the Divine Loving

Barth begins this section by affirming, "God's being is His loving" (II/1, 351). God is love, the one who loves us in his freedom. We can know this love only through grace because the very essence of God's being is also grace. "Fundamentally and decisively," Barth writes, "God distinguishes Himself from the creature by His grace" (II/1, 357). The creature, on the one hand, affirms the gracious nature of God, while simultaneously experiences God's resistance.

He further establishes divine perfections as:

1. Gracious and holy.
2. Merciful and righteous.

He defines mercy as "(. . .) therefore His compassion at the sight of the suffering which man brings upon himself, His concern to remove it, His will to console man in this pain and to help him to overcome it" (II/1, 372). And this mercy precedes righteousness, and grace precedes holiness. Coherently, he voices grace itself as mercy and merciful yet righteous, as seen in Jesus Christ. In other words, Jesus Christ embodies the answer to God's mercy and righteousness. It is indeed thought-provoking to observe Barth's prioritization of mercy and grace over righteousness and holiness, serving as advocates for the divine work that precedes our fruitful actions.

God chose to endure suffering for our sake in order to establish fellowship with us. "If we truly love Him," Barth asserts, "we must love Him also in His anger, condemnation and punishment (. . .)" (II/1, 394). Thus, God's mercy and righteousness manifested on the cross, as God is inherently love, mercy, grace, and patience through Jesus Christ. And the patience of God reflects his wisdom, which is an expression of his being and works (II/1, 432).

31. The Perfections of the Divine Freedom

God's freedom is an expression of his love and vice versa. His freedom is unlimited, as there is no other God alongside this God; one being in Jesus Christ. In his freedom, we see divine revelation in twofold aspects:

1. God chooses humans to reveal himself.
2. God chooses himself to reveal himself to humans (II/1, 450).

This twofold election is an election of choice, an event grounded in the love of God. For Barth, God's being is simultaneously distant and near to his creation. God's omnipresence is an external manifestation of who he is prior to and independent of creation. God "(. . .) is everywhere completely and undividedly the One He always is, even if the virtue of the freedom of His love" (II/1, 470). Furthermore, God created space because he possesses it, and we exist only within God's space. In general revelation, we see God's presence, but in special revelation, we see God's revelation and reconciliation in creation. Therefore, God's presence in the Word is God's revelation and reconciliation in Jesus Christ.

Barth argues that God created the world out of love and freedom, not out of necessity. God's relationship with the world is best understood as constancy, rather than immutability, as God is always loving and forgiving. This constancy is a divine secret that binds God to his creation. He remains himself as Father, Son, and the Holy Spirit with perfect and ultimate peace, despite the creation that lives in contradiction. God, in incarnation, became Jesus Christ, confirming his friendship with creation (II/1, 515). So, God, in revelation, took us up into fellowship through his will. "Everything that God knows He also wills, and everything that He wills He also knows" (II/1, 551). Even in our sins, we are within the gracious, holy, merciful, and righteous will of God. God's omnipotence is love, and everything flows from his active love and will (II/1, 599).

Barth concludes the chapter by establishing that eternity belongs to God alone, thereby underscoring the eternity of God. "The fact that Word became flesh," Barth argues, "undoubtedly means that, without ceasing to be eternity, in its very power as eternity, eternity became time" (II/1, 616). In other words, God became temporal in Jesus Christ without ceasing to be the triune God of eternity. God's glory is his power to act and will, yet he is beyond power. He says, "(. . .) the beginning, centre, and goal of these works of the divine glory is God's Son Jesus Christ" (II/1, 667). Therefore, our freedom to praise God lies in the revelation of this Word, Jesus Christ, the eternal center and destiny.

The Doctrine of God (Vol. II/2)

Chapter 7

The Election of God

32. The Problem of a Correct Doctrine of the Election of Grace

Barth's discussion on the doctrine of election starts with the statement, "It is grounded in the knowledge of Jesus Christ because He is both the electing God and electing man in One."[1] According to the holy Scriptures, Jesus Christ is the first and the last; hence, the doctrine of election should begin and end with him. It is through Jesus Christ that God chose to reveal himself to humanity, which expresses God's attitude of grace towards us. "God's decision," Barth writes, "in Jesus Christ is a gracious decision. In making it, God stoops down from above" (II/2, 10). In other words, God became the companion of humanity in Jesus Christ, in line with the foundational plan.

In his discourse with grace, Barth identifies that grace operates not only as a favor to be received and known but also as the will to rule. This rule of God's eternal election in grace is always a "yes," which precedes every human decision. God's election is characterized by freedom, mystery, and righteousness (II/2, 24). The divine elective love consistently endures as love; consequently, God has selected this mode of election through Jesus Christ. The

---

1. Barth, *Church Dogmatics* II/2, 2–3; hereafter cited as II/2.

creature cannot resist God's foreordination, which is his love and grace. Despite our "no," God is still "yes" for us in his grace. However, human freedom in election is found in God's freedom alone, not in themselves. According to Barth, "Our return to obedience is indeed the aim of free grace" (II/2, 30). And God's will in election is a "yes" for our salvation with no "ifs" and "buts." In other words, the "yes" has been actualized, and we need to recognize and acknowledge it.

He further examines the foundation of predestination in support of the fundamental principle of Church dogmatics, which asserts that all Christian doctrines are rooted in the holy Scriptures (II/2, 35). The holy Scriptures direct our attention to God as the primary individual in whom the election of grace has been established, specifically in reference to one man, Jesus Christ. He is the point of convergence in uniting the electing God and the elected human (II/2, 59). Thus, the doctrine of election is the head of all Christian dogmas. After all, God's eternal election has been bound with the virtue of his people because "(. . .) God is from the very first the gracious God" (II/2, 91). And humanity is not excluded from the realm of divine election or decision, whether at the pinnacle of creation or in the depths of sin. Therefore, the church should articulate not only its understanding of God himself, but also of all his ways and works.

33. The Election of Jesus Christ

Barth argues that Jesus Christ is the mediator of God's free grace to humanity. He is primarily the divine freedom and good pleasure of God's will and the original subject in the trinitarian election. Jesus Christ "(. . .) does not stand alongside the rest of the elect, but before and above them as One who is originally and properly the Elect" (II/2, 116). And the source of God's election is grace, where God empties himself of the divine form in transferring his love to the elect. "This is the radicalness of His grace" (II/2, 124), where "the triune God neither appears nor speaks to us except in the form of Jesus Christ (. . .)" (II/2, 150). This makes Jesus Christ the singular principle in the doctrine of election and forms the content of the whole Bible.

He further voices that God's election in Jesus Christ is a double predestination, where God loses himself in order that humans may gain (II/2, 162). God chose suffering and judgment grounded in his good pleasure so that he could become a friend to us. Barth defines, "Predestination means that God has determined, from all eternity, upon man's acquittal at His own cost" (II/2, 167). This cost is not a mixture of threat and joy; rather, it is purely joy in his relationship with humanity. God does not need humans, but he chose not to be without them; everything that happens in this world flows out of God's eternal decision that precedes all things (II/2, 185).

34. The Election of the Community

The election of grace in Jesus Christ can be identified as the eternal election of the one community of God, where the inner circle of the election—a community of believers—has taken place within the divine election. The objective of the election mediates through Israel and the church in its unity. He notices two poles of the elected community: on the one hand, humans turning away from the elected God, and on the other hand, the elected God turning towards humans.

He further argues that God's election of Jesus Christ is the election for the execution of God's judgment and mercy. And the church can never be estranged from the Israelites' story of suffering and redemption. "The church is the perfect form of the elected community of God" (II/2, 211). Consequently, Israel and the community of God coexist with their future and goal, as promised in Jesus Christ. God is not reliant upon Israel; rather, Israel exists for the purpose of eternal election. Therefore, Israel cannot oppose God but is bound to serve his will and work for his community (II/2, 263). In this manner, Israel accomplishes its universal mission by participating alongside the church.

35. The Election of the Individual

Barth transitions from community to individual election by hailing that what is determined in Jesus Christ is also determined for every individual, making Christian election more individualistic than secular individualism. According to him, this predestination is made acceptable to God through the work of the Holy Spirit. And humans can reject God, but they cannot reverse or annul God's decision (II/2, 317). So, the isolated human being has nowhere to go besides Jesus Christ, realizing "(. . .) that in Jesus Christ his rejection, too, is rejected, and his election consummated" (II/2, 322). Thus, despite their rejection, the elected and the rejected find their hope only in the election of Jesus Christ.

The elect may incur the rod, but not the sword of God. "God has made Him," Barth writes, "who is uniquely His Son and Friend, to be sin" (II/2, 352). As a result, the elect and the unelect are loved by God and stand alongside each other instead of against each other.

However, Barth observes an inseparable connection between the individual and the community election. The elect is summoned by the Holy Spirit, which encompasses the mission of sharing in the office of Jesus Christ (II/2, 415). And the responsibility of the elect is not to isolate themselves but to grow and expand in fulfilling their duties of word and deed. He contends that the death of Jesus Christ has terminated the rejection of the reject, while the resurrection has opened a place for the elect (II/2, 453). In sum, the message of Jesus' death and resurrection has paved the way for the future of all.

Chapter 8

The Command of God

36. Ethics as a Task of the Doctrine of God

Barth ventures into ethics by proposing it as the task of the doctrine of God. He asserts that the command of God is the beginning of every ethical question and answer. God's response to ethics lies in obedience to God's command, who alone is good. And the life of Jesus Christ fulfills the obedience of God's command because the Son is the only good that all other goods depend on.

He then shifts to the theological-ethical inquiry, which is justified by the command of God in the form of grace (II/2, 521). It is the command of God that distinguishes theological ethics from general moral ethics. Any attempt to establish general ethics as a basis for theological ethics is nothing but a destruction of theological ethics. In other words, theological ethics can only have command of the grace of God as the sole content and cannot be paired with philosophy and reason (II/2, 533). It is indeed the case that theological ethics must not be regarded as a perspective detached from the centrality of Jesus Christ. And God engages with humanity in this way because God himself is good.

37. The Command as the Claim of God

Barth begins this section by questioning, why is God the only commander for the claim on humans? "For God and God alone—above and inspite of all enmity to Him—is all—sufficient" (II/2, 555). Every divine claim fulfills the human claim, where we uphold God to uphold ourselves. In line with Luther, Barth speaks of the circle of faith, where God enters the circle by claiming humans, while humans accept the claim. This process of claiming is addressed through Jesus Christ, who dwells in us and leads us to the event where God claims us. In other words, God's command can only be searched and found in Jesus Christ.

"The fact that God is gracious to us," Barth argues, "does not mean that He becomes soft, but that He remains absolutely hard, that there is no escaping His sovereignty and therefore His purpose for man" (II/2, 560). Instead, the divine right of divine claim lies only in the gracious Lord Jesus Christ. So, obedience to God is always obedience to the gracious one, Jesus Christ. In discussing the profundity of Christ's love, Barth states, "however deep may be the ocean of that opposition within us, it is already drained to the depths in Jesus Christ" (II/2, 581).

Barth contends that God's command safeguards our freedom, as true happiness cannot be attained through our autonomous will. He observes a destructive dimension where, in freedom, we long for ourselves, yet we are against ourselves (II/2, 595). So, in God's command, humans are relieved of the fear of self-destruction and realize that God is not against them but for them. Indeed, the command comes in the form of the free love of God, grounded in divine freedom, through the act of his good pleasure. Thus, humans can fully exercise their freedom when they live under God's command rather than outside of it.

38. The Command as the Decision of God

Barth believed that our witness and conformity to God's command in Jesus Christ are essential. Because divine decisions are always superior to human decisions, and we are inseparably linked with God in the divine decisions to which we bear witness. If salvation is regarded as the work of Jesus Christ manifested through grace and goodness, what actions should be done from our perspective? Because even in our best actions, we are nothing but sorry and repentant in front of grace (II/2, 646). Barth answers that the 'ought' is meant to do the will of God joyfully in the virtue of the claim of the divine command that is beyond the human realm. In other words, in the ought, we are mere spectators, where we ought to allow our wills and aims to be confronted by the will of God as we meet his command. In sum, God's decision in Jesus Christ is the source of what we ought to decide as the responsible witnesses (II/2, 660).

However, the command of God comes to us as a demand, embracing the whole inner and outer substance of the totality of decision. In other words, the divine decision over us has been made in command, and our response, as a personal decision, is already included in God's command. Here, Barth affirms that the covenant of grace has a twofold dimension: where Christ's death is seen as a rejection of humans, while in his resurrection, God turned to humankind (II/2, 677). Thus, Jesus Christ is the good we are commanded to follow and bear witness to this will. And the command of God is God's good decision, which took place in the birth, life, death, and resurrection of Jesus Christ. Nevertheless, the command of God never allows humans to escape their responsibility.

39. The Command as the Judgment of God

Barth identifies that the "concept of God" is complete when we realize that God's judgment on humans is carried out through his command. We are summoned to stand in the light of God's judgment by God's yardstick because God, in his judgment, lives and rules in love (II/2, 735). In Jesus Christ, we encounter the judgment of God solely with joy, rather than fear. God bestows honor upon us through his command, irrespective of our attitude, as the essence of this command is grace (II/2, 747). Consequently, the mystery of grace can be unveiled only by the Holy Spirit.

In conclusion, Barth acknowledges that God's final judgment upon us goes beyond our sinfulness. God does not call evil good in the process of forgiveness; instead, God turns evil into good, as he calls the dead into life (II/2, 757). Evil undoubtedly contains no inherent good in it, but by the pure work of grace, God turns evil to good. And faith is an acknowledgment of the grace and mercy of God as an apprehension and affirmation of divine justification. As a result, a new human is born who can only do good works (II/2, 772). Therefore, God's purpose for our lives lies in God's judgment that has been fulfilled through Jesus Christ.

The Doctrine of Creation
(Vol. III/1)

Chapter 9

The Work of Creation

40. Faith in God the Creator

Barth begins volume three by exegeting the Apostle's Creed, specifically the first article: "I believe in God the Father Almighty, Maker of heaven and earth." He views the subsequent second and third articles as the most comprehensive exposition of the doctrine of creation for the church. He observes the relationship between the doctrine of creation and the doctrine of faith for the following reasons:

1. God created heaven, earth, and humans, which speaks of a reality distinct from God.
2. God's creation of heaven, earth, and humans asserts that this whole sphere is from God, which he willed and established for himself.
3. God calls the creator of heaven, earth, and humans, a concept that can be traced back to the linguistic usage in the holy Scriptures.

Regardless of the circumstances prevailing between God, the world, and humanity, the relationship between the creator and the creation reflects the inner life of the Father, the Son, and the Holy Spirit.

In the positive exposition of the relationship between the doctrine of creation and the doctrine of faith, Barth maintains that, in the light of Jesus Christ, the words of Scripture become the infallible Word of God.[1] In other words, the fundamental inquiries posed by the Bible receive their resolutions through the lens of Jesus Christ, and all necessary teachings from the Bible may be derived from this centrality of Jesus Christ. "We have established," Barth states, "from every angle Jesus Christ is the key to the secret of creation" (III/1, 28). And, the knowledge of creation is possible only through faith in Christ. Thus, the doctrine of creation is inseparable from the doctrine of faith because "Jesus Christ has established this right of the creator by reconciling the world with God" (III/1, 36).

41. Creation and Covenant

Barth recognizes that creation comes first in God's works, as he maintains it through transforming it through death, dissolution, and new creation, but never by destroying it. The Christian doctrine speaks of creation as a first cause and final contingency of the Father, Son, and the Holy Spirit. God the Father, as a creator, can be defended as the Father with the Son and the Holy Spirit. "In the respect of His Son who was to become man and the Bearer of human sin, God loved man and man's whole world from all eternity, even before it was created (. . .)" (III/1, 50). God's eternal love for the creation can be understood through the Son's eternal relationship with the Father and the Holy Spirit. And the creation is more closely attributed to the Son, as he is the subject and object of the creation.

Creation represents a historical account of a covenant of grace established by God with humanity, enacted through events that God both ordains and executes throughout eternity. "By beginning with the story of creation the Bible protects the faith in God to which it invites and summons from being regarded (. . .) as special sphere of reality" (III/1, 62). The historical reality of the

---

1. Barth, *Church Dogmatics* III/1, 23; hereafter cited as III/1.

biblical account hails God's grace as a paramount principle, which God willed, created, and revealed in his relationship with humankind. It can be observed that without the grace of God, he will not give himself the ability to enter into the form of human existence and to have a relationship with the creation. The creator-creation relationship can be best understood through the lens of the covenantal relationship.

Barth delves further into the creation story by defining creation history as a saga and not a myth. It is a pure saga distinguished from mere history (as it has deeper metaphysical and ethical aspects) on one side and mythical aspects on the other. The biblical creation saga adopts a narrative form that invites readers to engage with the story, appreciating its events and the eternal truths presented therein. "The biblical creation saga," Barth writes, "speaks in this way without nods or winks, without irony (. . .) its divination and poetry are intended to say exactly what it says in itself and in this connexion" (III/1, 86). Therefore, the biblical creation stories are not "heaven-sent declarations" of the truth that dropped from the sky, but rather "human attestations" given within the creaturely sphere. In this context, one can observe Barth's attentiveness to Scripture as it manifests in human expressions in right tension to the veracity of God's truth.

He believes that a creature's right, meaning, goal, purpose, and dignity lie only in God, the creator, who turned toward the creature with his purpose. "God loves His own creature. This is absolutely unique feature of the covenant in which His love is exercised and fulfilled" (III/1, 96). The creation demonstrates God's plan, as the theatre of God's acts, which can be seen in God's image in human beings, reflecting God's nature as the one who knows, wills, and speaks. And the separation of light and waters signifies the transformation of chaos into the cosmos, indicating God's order in creation. Finally, humans appear to be the center of creation, making them the most "necessitous of all creatures." In other words, humans are invited and admitted to the table that the Lord prepared for them to dine and inhabit.

THE DOCTRINE OF CREATION (VOL. III/1)

In creating fish, birds, and animals, we see them as sharing in humans' animal nature, where the humans and animal creation bear witness to this covenant (III/1, 171). However, humans alone are created in the image of God and honored to be God's partner in the covenant of grace. And the sixth day of creation marks the point of created order, where God reflects on his work, while the seventh day is the day of his rest. In accordance with the biblical text, Barth asserts that humans are undoubtedly the crown of creation, bearing God's image, which establishes the ground and possibility of human living within God's sphere, not outside of it.

Venturing further into the God-human relationship, Barth observes that no one in creation can stand face-to-face with God in an I-Thou relationship except for humans. He defines humans simply as male and female, "(. . .) God did not create man alone, as a single human being, but in the unequal duality of male and female" (III/1, 188). According to Barth, humans are invariably and always categorized as female and male in all differentiations. Any other differentiation will be supplementary to this fact. In addition, Barth distinguishes humans from animals in three ways:

1. Humans and animals should be nourished by the vegetable kingdom.
2. Humans are the first to be invited to the table of everything in creation, and only then the animals.
3. God intended only plants to be the food and not animals.

And the Sabbath is to follow what God did on the Sabbath: he rested from further creative work. The rest can be seen in two ways: primarily through the Sabbath, where God revealed the feature of his freedom by resting on the seventh day, and secondly, God revealed in the rest his love for himself and the creature, who is satisfied with his work. Notably, Barth delves into a profound insight into God's primordial love for himself as expressed through the day of rest. He also believes that the Sabbath is a promise given to humans to follow at the beginning of the working week; before our merits and work, we are invited to share in God's freedom, rest, and joy. Thus, the creature exists meaningfully in realizing its purpose, plan, and order.

What God created is not just perfect, but to be a partner in his grace, willed to address humans as those who are predestined for his service. "It is man and man alone," Barth affirms, "who becomes a living soul in this way" (III/1, 236). Thus, humans are commissioned to serve, work, and maintain the earth, making them responsible to God and the creation.

He observes that the second story of creation deals with the Garden of Eden, its trees, rivers, and the permissions and prohibitions given to humans. And when humans transgress God's prohibition, they will die, and the process of life will be changed into death, return to dust, and the removal of the soul. "Unlike God's," Barth writes, "man's decision will be a decision for evil, destruction and death: not because he is man, but because he is only man and not God (. . .)" (III/1, 261). This indicates that even though humans are perceived as the crown of the creation, they can never be equated with God and his character. In addition, the existence of the Tree of Knowledge of Good and Evil and its prohibition underscores humans' ability to make personal decisions to obey. This obedience is possible through God-given wisdom and righteousness, which are the two mighty wings that give freedom to obey. Thus, "He gives him freedom to obey, and has not therefore made obedience physically necessary or disobedience physically impossible" (III/1, 266). The concept of necessary obedience, despite the impossibility of disobedience, is where we see Barth's dialectical play of God's sovereignty over every human will.

He further argues that Eden is different from Cannon and its location remains unknown. He symbolically considers Eden to be a place of God's grace, where the two trees at the center represent the Gospel and Law. Human beings must actively seek, find, accept, and acknowledge God's help. "Apart from this act of human freedom, the supreme and final gift of God would not be what it is" (III/1, 291). Adam's failure to find a helpmeet is not a failure of divine experiment. Indeed, God had to act this way so that humans would recognize, choose, and confirm the helpmeet ordained and created by God.

"God used man," Barth writes, "for the creation of woman just as He used the dust of the earth for the creation of man. In both cases He fashioned the new out of the old" (III/1, 297). And God created woman and man not just as "I and Thou" but to live in a mutual relationship. The creation of woman from man does not denote the superiority of man, but that man can fully partake of his lost part of his own body by partaking in woman. In observing this episode, Barth articulates, "What is meant by the statement that woman 'was taken out of Man' is that God willed to complete man of and through himself irrespective of any capacity of his own" (III/1, 302). As a result, in marriage, the man must be the one who seeks sacrifices and is utterly dependent on the woman to fulfill his relationship. Indeed, he is the weaker half because all this is rooted and grounded in divine will and purpose. Therefore, the subordination of women was only an expression of help that did "not involve any humiliation for her" (III/1, 309).

42. The Yes of God the Creator

Barth believes that God's creation carries with it the "Yes" of God to that which he created. "Creation as such," Barth argues, "is not rejection, but election and acceptance. It is God's positing in accordance with His nature of a reality which is distinct from Him but willed by Him" (III/1, 331). The "Yes" of God can be understood when seen from the lens of creation and covenant, which acknowledges that God, as the creator in Jesus Christ, has affirmed his creation by not only actualizing it but also justifying it.

Barth further believed that Christ's self-revelation binds us to love and appreciate the created order and upholds him as the mystery of God's being, unknown to us. He affirms that the Christian faith lives by the "Yes" that God himself has spoken for joy and peace and "No" to the danger threatening from the sphere of nothingness. Therefore, "we are not mere hearers of the divine revelation. We are ourselves its witnesses" (III/1, 388). It is noteworthy that in the context of the threat, Barth introduces the concept of nothingness, which will be discussed in greater length in the upcoming sections (paragraphs).

The Doctrine of Creation
(Vol. III/2)

Chapter 10

The Creature

43. Man as a Problem of Dogmatics

Barth elucidates that the entirety of the cosmos constitutes the creation to which humans belong. Humans are equally bound and committed to both heaven and earth. And the Word of God, which is the object of church dogmatics, always contains a specific cosmology that needs to be expounded as follows.

1. Faith that grasps the Word of God witnesses itself in cosmologies.
2. The biblical worldview speaks of humans in relation to their lives under heaven and earth.
3. Faith, committed to its theme, gives only incidental attention to cosmological presuppositions.
4. Even when dealing with faith, we are dealing only with partial deviation from faith by dealing only with necessary Christian faith.
5. Even in conjunction with faith, our associations with other worldviews stand in opposition.

In other words, "The Word of God," Barth says, "has a cosmological border. It illuminates the world. It makes heaven and earth known as the sphere in which God's glory dwells and in which He concerns Himself with man."[1] Even though dogmatics has no business broadening into cosmology, it has a responsibility to expound on the doctrine of humans. This is why Barth thinks that the doctrine of the human has always been central to the dogmatics of the creature. The cosmos surrounding humans is not independent but the will and work of the Creator, which reflects his glory. Therefore, God's covenant with humans also includes that the cosmos is part of the same covenant (III/2, 19).

Theological anthropology clings to the Word of God and the biblical attestation because "the Word of God is thus its foundation" (III/2, 20). However, Barth acknowledges that "Scientific anthropology gives us precise information and relevant data which can be of service in the wider investigation of the nature of man (. . .)" (III/2, 26). But "Only by the Word does he know that while he is a sinner he is not merely a sinner, but that even as sinner he is God's creature and as such real before God" (III/2, 31). Although Barth presents human beings in juxtaposition to grace, he maintains that the covenant between God and humanity retains primacy in this relationship, while human sin is considered a secondary aspect. In other words, God is open to the creation in grace through Jesus Christ, the Word of God.

In the context of theological anthropology, Barth opines that we should inquire about the nature of humans in relation to the revealed grace of God in Jesus Christ. Jesus alone is our ambassador, through whom our sins are rightfully removed and destroyed. As a result, Jesus' pure humanity has been imputed as our humanity. Thus, "Jesus is utterly unlike us as God and utterly like us as man is the twofold fact which constitutes the whole secret of His person" (III/2, 53). Jesus' humanity is thus a mystery that binds the essence of humanity with God in an indissoluble unity.

---

1. Barth, *Church Dogmatics* III/2, 11; hereafter cited as III/2.

44. Man as the Creature of God

Barth points to Jesus' life and work as the real human who suffered and died as the saviour of the world. "For this reason," Barth voices, "we cannot separate His person from His work-as should now be clearer" (III/2, 61). When we see the essence of humans through Jesus, we realize that humans are essentially created from and for God (III/2, 71).

But this real man, Jesus, is different from the other beings and cannot merge into his environment, as he would cease to be the real man because "to 'exist' is to 'step out' (...)" (III/2, 92). However, Jesus' existence is in relationship to another being, and yet he transcends the natural and ethical life. And "it is always in this act of self-transcendence that he exists properly and concretely" (III/2, 110). Similarly, human existence is transformed from mere possibility to reality when faced with "frontier situations" such as suffering, death, guilt, etc. "It is such crises which really brings man into relation with the wholly other, and lead him to an existence which embodies the meaning of this relation" (III/2, 114). In other words, a human exists only in relation to God, necessarily and essentially.

In pressing forward with the doctrine of sin, Barth perceives sin not as a possibility but as an ontological impossibility for humans. But in Jesus, our being does not include sin but excludes it because "(...) Jesus as the Bearer of the divine uniqueness and transcendence is like man, God is revealed to man, and in this confrontation with God man is revealed to himself" (III/2, 138). In conclusion, it is solely through Jesus that we, as human beings, attain a profound understanding of our identity; our relationship with Jesus holds greater significance than sin.

On contrary, he identifies a monstrous kingdom, "a deep chaos of nothingness, i.e., of what the Creator has excluded and separated from the sphere of being, of what He did not will and therefore did not create, to which He gave no being, which can exist only as a non-being (...)" (III/2, 143). Barth's view on evil as nothingness with words such as, "did not create," "He gave no being" and "can exist only as a non-being," indicates that he believed that there is already something that is existing out of which, God called forth only something and made a creation. However, it remains dubious how he interpreted the biblical creation account of *ex nihilo*.

He further explains that God did not intend for humans to fall, but it was not out of his foresight and plan. When humans choose evil, they choose it from what is made impossible for them and from which they are preserved. Ultimately, "God takes up the cause of the threatened creature, that in the midst of creation God guards man and appoints him a guardian" (III/2, 163). Thus, the inception of human beings is set in motion by the fact that God is gracious to threatened humanity, and nothing can surprise the sovereign God. And the human counterpart to the grace of God is gratitude, "We may thus say that the being of man is a being in gratitude" (III/2, 167). Barth furthers the aspect of gratitude as the relationship between God and humans in the following ways:

1. Only God deserves the gratitude of humans.
2. God can only be thanked by humans among the whole creation
3. Humans fulfill their true being as they thank God.
4. Humans are obligated to thank God.

He also identifies the following aspects that we characterize as responsible beings before God as follows:

1. We embody the knowledge of God.
2. We are characterized by obedience to God.
3. We invoke God.
4. We possess the freedom imparted by God.

The general knowledge may provide some enlightenment; however, it evaluates human phenomena from a simplistic self-understanding, which the "theological anthropology is prepared to welcome all such general knowledge of man" (III/2, 202).

45. Man in His Determination as the Covenant-Partner of God

Barth states that "real man lives with God as His covenant-partner" (III/2, 203). So, he presents two essential ways of viewing humans: as covenant partners and their cosmic and creaturely being. The covenant relationship cannot be annulled by human sin or replaced by humanity in a different reality. Instead, our understanding of humanity should be based on the humanity of Jesus. He proposes that we should first consider the humanity of Jesus and then use that as a basis to explore the nature of humanity in general. Because "the Word and grace of God are exclusively at work in Him and by Him" (III/2, 208). Jesus, in his humanity, reflects the inner being of God as Father, Son, and Holy Spirit. And through the inconceivable grace, God took Jesus to himself so "(. . .) that in the fellow-humanity of Jesus the free choice of the divine will is revealed and exercised as love for man" (III/2, 224).

He furthers his argument by affirming that "being with" means "encounter." The "(. . .) being in encounter is a being in the openness of the one to the other with a view to and on behalf of the other" (III/2, 250). He proposes four elements in the human openness:

1. Gazing into the other person's eyes.
2. Engaging in mutual speech and listening.
3. Providing mutual assistance to each other in existence.
4. Mutually carrying all occurrences with joy.

"The secret of his humanity," Barth states, "however is that in his being in the encounter of I and Thou we do not have to do with a determination (. . .) but with a self-determination which is free and intrinsic to his essence" (III/2, 267). In other words, humans possess an openness and self-determination through their mutual relationship with God, which is made possible through Jesus Christ.

For Barth, the real human is the one who lives with their fellow human, where their freedom is intended to seek the other. In other words, the basic form of humanity is fellow humanity. In setting the basic premise firmly, he progresses to reestablish humanity primarily as male and female. And the relationship between woman and man can be achieved when they mutually love each other "(. . .) in free choice and with a view to a full life-partnership (. . .)" (III/2, 288). "For man without the fellow-man," Barth writes, "would be a creature which has nothing in common with the man Jesus, and with which the man Jesus has nothing in common" (III/2, 317). Therefore, God, who lives in the relationship as the Trinity, chose to create human beings in this relationship and in the divine likeness, where humans live in mutual relationship with one another.

46. Man as Soul and Body

Barth articulates the essence of human existence through the concept of the soul residing within the human body. "Man's being exists, and is therefore soul; and it exists in a certain form, and is therefore body" (III/2, 325). He lists a few aspects to consider when considering our humanity in light of Jesus' humanity. The first thing to note about the human nature of Jesus is his oneness and wholeness, while the second is to understand that this human life is shaped, structured, and determined from within (III/2, 332). "Soul and body are clearly related to one another in the man Jesus, as His being as Son and Word of God the Creator is related to His creaturely constitution as soul and body of this man" (III/2, 341).

Humans exist because they have a spirit that is grounded and maintained by God as the soul of their bodies. There is an asymmetrical relation between soul and body: the "Soul would not be soul, if it were not bodily; and body would not be body, if it were not besouled" (III/2, 350). Along with soul and body, "he is, as the spirit has him" (III/2, 354). Then what is Spirit? It is nothing but "the principle of man's relation to God, of man's fellowship with Him" (III/2, 356). It appears that for Barth, spirit is not an extrinsic element to body and soul; instead, it is a relational aspect that is inseparable from the body and soul. The soul is a spiritual and non-spatial one, which "(. . .) the Spirit that unifies him and holds him together as soul and body" (III/2, 393). The soul is also referred to as self-consciousness. In addition, he says that an animal has a spirit, but we are unaware of what that means to an animal.

47. Man in His Time

In the context of creation, Barth emphasizes the necessity of time for a being to fulfill its functions, both as a soul and a body. He recounts Jesus as the "Lord of time" (III/2, 440). We see Jesus in time and history from his birth to death. At the same time, the resurrected Jesus in post-history appeared to the disciples, "But their doubts and disbelief are soon dispelled, never to return. They are definitively overcome and removed in the forty days" (III/2, 449). In other words, the post-resurrection episodes of Jesus also signify that he appeared in the post-history. "It is the Creator," Barth states, "of all reality distinct from Himself who taking flesh of our flesh, also took time, at the heart of what we think we know as time" (III/2, 455). The Son, who has been living eternally (pre-history), chose to come down and live as Jesus Christ (history), and has also appeared after his resurrection (post-history), claiming that he is Lord over time and history.

    He further distinguishes Jesus' time from other times as three-dimensional: as every other time begins, has a duration, and finally comes to an end (III/2, 463). But Jesus "(. . .) is the same yesterday, and today," and yet "(. . .) His real and supreme and full and divine past cannot conflict with His being in the future" (III/2, 477). Those forty days of post-resurrection appearances point to the anticipation of Parousia. "Even in eternal life," Barth writes, "he (humans) will still be in his time" (III/2, 521). However, eternity is not timelessness; "it is beginning, middle and end in fulness, for it is all three simultaneously" (III/2, 558). It "(. . .) is the dimension of God's own life, the life (. . .) as Father, Son, and Holy Ghost" (III/2, 526). In Jesus, God is eternal in two ways:

1. God in eternity is not far from us but near to us.
2. God is not hidden from us in eternity but has manifested as the Lord of time.

Barth's concept of eternity and time is mysterious and can only be apprehended and pointed to the mystery of Christ alone.

God established human existence to foster relationships with himself and with one another. This purpose endures, even in instances where humanity falters and rejects its inherent nature in both regards. It is assumed that God exists not solely for himself but has, through his grace, turned his attention towards us. This gracious God is not an abstraction but the concrete reality, embodied in Jesus, who is the master of time and history. Thus, "(. . .) a definite anthropology results from Christology" (III/2, 571).

At our inception, we transitioned from nonexistence to existence, signifying our ultimate positivity, which originates from God. But when we die, we come to an end, and the finitude of our time becomes critically limited (III/2, 588). "It is in this irreparable state of transgression," Barth voices, "that we shall be translated from being to non-being and brought face to face with our Creator" (III/2, 596). In other words, death can be seen as a sign of God's judgment. Nevertheless, the good news in the rule of death is that "it is really our nothingness (. . .) but this is to say that at the point where we shall be at our end, it is not merely death but God Himself who awaits us" (III/2, 608). "Even in hell," Barth states, "we shall be in His hands. Even in its torments we shall be shielded with Him (. . .)" and even "if the fire of his wrath scorches us, it is because it is the fire of His wrathful love and not His wrathful hate" (III/2, 609). It is noteworthy that Barth does not relinquish hope, even in the face of hell and torment, and that his wheels of the dialectical theology are undoubtedly fueled by the grace imparted through Jesus Christ.

The Doctrine of Creation
(Vol. III/3)

Chapter 11

The Creator and His Creature

48. The Doctrine of Providence, Its Basis and Form

Barth begins this section on the one hand by recounting the post-Reformation dogmatics view of the doctrine of providence in close relation to the doctrine of creation. On the other hand, he grounds the doctrine of providence in the being of God. He distinguishes creation as an establishment, while providence is a continuation, establishing a reciprocal relationship between the two doctrines. "We cannot think of the one without the other," Barth argues, because "(. . .) the obvious reason for this is that the one does not occur without the other."[1]

The Creator and the creature are addressed in the eternal counsel to establish the covenant between God and human beings. "The doctrine of providence," Barth writes, "must not level down the special history of the covenant, grace and salvation (. . .)" instead, it "presupposes that this special history is exalted above all other history" (III/3, 37). And God shapes this covenant history following the eternal counsel through the provision of grace.

---

1. Barth, *Church Dogmatics* III/3, 9; hereafter cited as III/3.

THE DOCTRINE OF CREATION (VOL. III/3)

49. God the Father as Lord of His Creature

God sustains his creature with mercy revealed through Jesus Christ in creaturely form. In Jesus Christ, God has become "(. . .) the pledge and guarantee of its creaturely existence (. . .)" (III/3, 60). He has preserved not only the creature but also its covenantal context. Here, Barth purports the covenant context to the church by stating that "the church is either a missionary Church or it is no church at all. And Christians are either the messengers of God (with or without words) to both Jew and Gentile or else they are not Christians at all" (III/3, 64). Barth contends that the church and the Christian must always live and strive towards the covenantal relationship.

He further proposes that the creation is "appointed" to live and triumph by the grace of God. Only the nothingness to which God said "No" stands in a dialectical relationship to God's "Yes" that finds its power in the wrath of God (III/3, 77). To redeem us from this wrath, God entered through the inside by taking our place and facing the "all-powerful negation" of our being. He further affirms that God accompanies the creature in the following ways:

1. God accompanies the creature not merely as once in activity but every moment—"momentary preservation."
2. In the process, God upholds the autonomous activity of the creature.
3. God walks along the creature in cooperation with it (III/3, 93).

In the Creator-creature relationship, love is primary as "the creature can only be loved by God, and then at best love Him in return" (III/3, 107). God chose this relationship as an inward necessity in love and accompanies the creature in his good pleasure. In other words, God executes the covenant history through the decree of grace.

Barth proceeds with his discourse in moving to the concept of divine foreordination, stating that it "(. . .) takes place before and above all the other foreordinations and determinations (. . .)" (III/3, 130). He contends that God's activity and creatures' activity are a single action mediated by the work of the Holy Spirit. The whole activity ought to be credited to this jealous God, who is jealous not because there are competitors, "(. . .) but because of His loving zeal for the creature that He retains to Himself the control of all things and will not and cannot share it with another" (III/3, 159). "(. . .) God does actually control creaturely activity (. . .) but God controls the activity in its freedom no less than its necessity. The control of God is transcendent" (III/3, 165). This draws us closer to the fact that God not only sets the goals for the creature but also strengthens it to attain them, as we see in the continuity of the Old and the New Testaments, as an "all-powerful Word" and "all-powerful act," respectively, on the same path. As a result, Barth admonishes that we cannot approach the witnesses of the prophets and apostles, i.e., Scripture, as mere objects of study, but they always speak to us afresh at every age. The proclaimed Word of God in the church is new every morning and renews us day after day.

However, the doctrine of providence is an integral part of Christian confession. A genuine Christian understanding is rooted in the comprehension of divine providence and the overarching sovereignty of God. In this context, he offers three forms of Christian attitudes to the divine providence and lordship:

1. Faith is the source of the Christian attitude that summons the whole heart, soul, mind, and strength.
2. Obedience to the Word of God.
3. Prayer as the primary aspect of faith and obedience.

"Therefore Christian prayer," Barth writes, "is inevitably a confession of his own weakness and inability and unworthiness, of the whole lost condition in which he is discovered in the sight of God" (III/3, 267). In other words, prayer precedes faith and obedience, and the Son of God is "the divine gift and answer" to human asking. In prayer, the Christian transcends her limitations and turns to God as the one who confronts us in mercy. And in obedience, the Christian is the servant, but in prayer, she is the friend of God (III/3, 286).

50. God and Nothingness

Barth addresses an "alien factor" that cannot escape God's providence. He defines this opposing factor as "nothingness." "It is true that in creation," Barth writes, "there is not only a Yes but also a No; no only a height but also abyss (. . .) not only beauty but also ashes; not only beginning but also end; not only value but also worthlessness" (III/3, 297). He proposes that nothingness should be understood as a distinct aspect of creation that stands as the harmful content to God and no less to us as his creation; a reality that opposes and resists God. Indeed, it is this reality that brought Jesus to the cross, where it was ultimately defeated. "Only from the standpoint of Jesus Christ, His birth, death and resurrection, do we see it in reality and truth (. . .)" (III/3, 305). Even though sin is perceived as the concrete form of nothingness, it cannot be exhausted in sin alone.

The source of nothingness can be noticed when God elected the creation, "(. . .) and therefore rejects what He does not elect (. . .) He says Yes, and therefore says No to that to which He has not said Yes" (III/3, 351). This informs us that nothingness lives by the fact that God did not will it. And it only lives as an emptiness with no substance (III/3, 361). Even though God abandoned nothingness once and for all, the creation remains vulnerable to the manifestation of its brokenness until its complete victory is revealed in Jesus Christ. In other words, Barth understands that Christ would ultimately conquer the full force of nothingness in the future course of an action.

51. The Kingdom of Heaven, the Ambassadors of God and Their Opponents

In the kingdom of heaven, God sends messengers, the angels, to carry forward his will. To further our inquiry into angels, Barth proposes that we hold firm to the "Scripture-principle" instead of tradition. "In this matter of angels," Barth writes, "we must dare to trust the Holy Spirit, and for good or evil we must dare to trust

Him alone" (III/3, 403). However, the biblical account lacks sufficient details regarding the nature of angels, as they exist outside the realm of earthly matters.

The kingdom of God, as Barth understands, comes to us as the kingdom of heaven in "(. . .) multiplicity of revelations and declarations, of events and relationships, of individuals and societies, which have their constitutive center in God Himself, namely, in Jesus Christ as very God and very man (. . .)" (III/3, 448). This kingdom encompasses dialectical aspects such as universality-particularity, totality-multiplicity, and collectively-individually. The angels are recognized as original witnesses of the Word of God, but they cannot carry out divine works on their own, nor can they save, redeem, or liberate the earth's creatures. "Their ministry is a ministry of witness (. . .) His primary, authentic, constant, inflexible, and infallible witnesses" (III/3, 462). So, the words and works of angels can be considered to be those of God, as God speaks through them.

Barth even goes so far as to say that to deny the angels is to deny God himself. At the same time, he also says God needs no mediators as "He Himself throws a bridge across the gulf, and secures it on both sides" (III/3, 495). Angels have no deviation from God as they are "perfect witnesses" of him. But are they witnesses of all ages? In response, Barth contends that the ministry of angels is not confined to a specific historical moment; rather, it exists throughout the covenant history, allowing humans to participate alongside the angels across all ages.

Nevertheless, the angels are the creation and manifestation of God's grace, while demons are chaotic, embodying nothingness, evil, and myth. Demons and devils find their origin in the nothingness and hence not in God's creation. But "it too is undoubtedly superior to man and the whole earthly creation. It, too has its midst a kind of throne and ruler (. . .) We cannot deny the power and powers of falsehood in a thousand different forms" (III/3, 527). Thus, he concludes biblical demonology is a negative reflection that stands in contradiction to Christology and soteriology. It is particularly noteworthy to understand the manner in which Barth articulates that nothingness is regarded as superior to humanity and creation. Holding both a throne and a ruler implies that, under no circumstances, can we consider nothingness as powerless.

The Doctrine of Creation
(Vol. III/4)

Chapter 12

The Command of God the Creator

52. Ethics as a Task of the Doctrine of Creation

Barth understands ethics as the pursuit of good actions carried out in mutual cooperation between God and humanity. He distinguishes general ethics from special ethics, defining general ethics as that "which forms part of the doctrine of God as counterpart to the doctrine of election."[1] Special ethics involves following God's command, which is partly expressed in the biblical texts and partly through the "(. . .) natural moral law generally perceptible to human reason (. . .)" (III/4, 6). We can observe that Barth believes in the natural moral law inherent in human beings to some extent.

He delves deeper into the relationship between ethics and dogmatics, emphasizing their subordination to the divine command. According to Barth, the divine command confronts sinful humans, exalting them through God's faithfulness, leading to human action. "The God who commands," Barth writes, "is also the Reconciler and the Redeemer, and something corresponding may also be said of man with whom He has to deal in this event" (III/4, 28). It is this event where God commands, and humans act. Dogmatics should invariably encompass ethics, and both dogmatics

---

1. Barth, *Church Dogmatics* III/4, 4; hereafter cited as III/4.

and ethics ought to be carried out by humans under the illumination of revelation.

The God who meets us in the revelation of Jesus Christ is none other than the gracious God. "The eternal decree of God," Barth states, "which precedes creation and makes it possible and necessary is the gracious election of man in Jesus Christ" (III/4, 39). Thus, humans cannot understand themselves except by seeing through the gracious mirror of Jesus Christ. For Barth, the real meaning of human life and ethics can only be drawn from the revelation of Jesus Christ.

53. Freedom Before God

Human beings, whether willingly or capriciously, are drawn to surrender themselves wholly to God in obedience. Indeed, the command of the sabbath is to aim "(. . .) at this complete surrender and capitulation by singling out one day (. . .)" (III/4, 54). The command is holistic in nature, further stretching into the physical, psychological, and social realms. Human freedom can be observed in confessions. He defines Confession as a "(. . .) liberation by the heartfelt declaration of a strong religious experience or emotion (. . .) that a man dares to give honor to God" (III/4, 78). However, confession cannot be of an individual nature; it is entrusted to the community by the Word of God, which is heard and proclaimed. And it is a free choice in obedience that proceeds from the work of the Holy Spirit.

Barth identifies an inseparable relationship with the confession, stating that humans are recipients in relation to God, but in prayer, humans present themselves as an application directed to God. "Prayer and confession are related in respect of their common basis in the knowledge of God, like breathing in and breathing out, systole and diastole" (III/4, 88). The true prayer finds itself in thanksgiving, repentance, and worship. However, he critiques mechanical prayer by stating, "better no prayer at all than the operation of this kind of mechanism" (III/4, 113).

54. Freedom in Fellowship

Barth posits that humanity is summoned to freedom within the context of fellowship, as it serves as the foundation of humankind; conversely, it remains inhumanity. The point is further driven to the woman and man's relationship where man "(. . .) wish to liberate himself from the relationship and be man without woman or woman apart from man; for in all that characterises him as man he will be thrown back upon woman, or as woman upon man, both man and woman being referred to this encounter and coexistence" (III/4, 118). And this co-existence cannot be limited to sexual needs, but to the order and sequence of the human being.

The relationship between a woman and a man is centered on marriage. And all other relationships find their ground in marriage. God has created human beings in this either-or, as male or female, and we have to acknowledge our sexes as they are rather than to be ashamed of them (III/4, 149). Indeed, God's special gift, coupled with the duty for humans, is indicated in the command of God as female and male. Man and woman, as he sees them, are "two halves of an hourglass," emphasizing their equality and interchangeability before God and society. However, Barth has a subtle forward move for man to woman as he understands that man cannot be glorified over woman; instead, he is directed to woman in "(. . .) taking the lead as the inspirer, leader, and initiator" in their common action (III/4, 170). In other words, "(. . .) he is first and she second is valid and effective particularly in this sphere" (III/4, 193). While Barth displays considerable insight into the dynamics of femininity and masculinity, it is regrettable that he does not appear to have advanced beyond the confines of a patriarchal perspective.

He further delves into marriage being the ideal relationship in voicing that "here all the lines intersect which elsewhere only converge and in many instances break off without reaching this point" (III/4, 182). Marriage can only be fully understood when viewed as being placed under divine command. Marriage is a life partnership that is beyond sexual needs, creating a home, an institution of procreation, and so on. However, Barth also grounds marriage on the choice made on love and "hence it is monogamy" (III/4, 195). Marriage, thus, is an archetypal form of fellowship that reflects the image and likeness of God.

Barth further develops his argument by stating that the marriage relationship is akin to that of parent and child. Through divine grace, the children are commanded to submit to their parents. But God alone can offer the "(. . .) true Wisdom, and therefore the true Teacher, Guide and Educator" (III/4, 247). Barth views parents not only as authority figures but as no more than senior friends with their limitations. He affirms that parenthood, in some sense, is an optional gift of God's goodness because "it certainly cannot be a fault to be without children" (III/4, 266). He even goes the extra mile in critiquing that, at times, children may be a serious threat to the marriage and the surrounding people. Nevertheless, the parents ought to align themselves as God's representatives to their children.

55. Freedom for Life

Barth posits that our existence as human beings is not solely our own but rather loaned to us, as God assures us that our lives possess a definitive origin solely in him (III/4, 329). Human life finds its dignity when seen through the lens of Jesus Christ, who reveals the eternal election of God in love. "Human life" for Barth, "must be considered as given by God for specific purpose and set under His special protection, and therefore it must be treated with holy awe" (III/4, 344). In this sphere, humans recognize their fundamental responsibility for their neighbors and also to act responsibly towards non-human life. On the contrary, sickness is a real encroachment on life with the power to impair the functions of the soul and body, resulting in life as a fallen victim to nothingness (III/4, 372). While "joy is really the simplest form of gratitude" (III/4, 376).

Within the freedom of life, Barth now ventures into the negation of suicide. "Suicide," Barth writes, "is a last and most radical means of procuring for oneself justice and freedom" (III/4, 403).

Deprivation of human life belongs to the Creator and not to the creature. The person who is assailed by the void is the one who toys with the thought of self-destruction. In other words, "self-destruction does not have to be the taking of one's own life. Its meaning and intention might well be a definite if extreme form of the self-offering required of man" (III/4, 410). In sum, suicide is a lust that has gone out of control, resulting in murder.

On the same tone, he stretches the argument to abortion in viewing the unborn child cannot be treated as a thing or a mere part of the mother's body, but as an individual human being. We have no right to decide on behalf of the unborn child and thus cannot be justified before the command of God. Similarly, on the capital punishment, Barth questions, "What right has society to let one of its members fall, to declare itself incapable of having further contact with him, and thus to maintain that it is justified in breaking off this contact once and for all and irrevocably?" (III/4, 441). He acknowledges that the death sentence for all human criminals has already been imposed once and for all on Jesus Christ. In this light, just judgment can only be "mercy and forgiveness for all." Understandably, Barth views human life as a gracious gift and evades any argument for shortening it under any circumstances.

The central concern with capital punishment is that it cuts off God's allotted period for a human being who may repent for their past. "If the command to protect life is accepted and asserted in some sense in a national community, then it is impossible to maintain capital punishment as an element in its normal and continuing order" (III/4, 445). He comments that the Christian Church has failed to voice against capital punishment and has become "savourless salt." Similarly, Barth asserts that all that a war requires is what God has prohibited for human life. He instead advocates for peace as a real emergency, enabling human lives to be lived to their fullest potential. However, the church "(. . .) in the rare case of a just war, to tell men that, even though they now have to kill, they are not murderers, but may and must do the will of God in this *opus alienum* of the state" (III/4, 464). And the church, in obedience to the command, at times may take an opposite view to the state.

He recounts that human life cannot be isolated, but rather lives in conjunction with fellow humans and their environment. The command of God demands an active life where she lives and acts with the aim of accomplishing it. "An active life," Barth affirms, "lived in obedience must obviously consist in a correspondence to divine action" (III/4, 474). Jesus Christ sets this active life in motion, and the church functions efficiently as people live actively. He asserts that a person "(. . .) cannot be a Christian without being in the community. Hence, he will constantly orient his life by that of the community and its other members" (III/4, 496). In its active life, the church, as a community, is called to represent God's love and to declare salvation to the world. Barth reestablishes, "The community is as such a missionary community or it is not the Christian community. Again, each individual is responsible for its actually being a missionary community" (III/4, 505). A community with a mission has to actively work together to earn a living and share it with fellow workers.

Along the same lines, Barth critiques capitalism, which wheels on injustice in the development of labor. On the contrary, he proposes that the Christian community should have advocated for the proclamation of God's kingdom over socialism, which stands against every ungodliness and unrighteousness (III/4, 545). He further explores championing the criterion for rest in stating that "the demanded rest from all his labor is that he should do his work with diligence but also with the recollection that God is Lord, Master, Provider (. . .) and therefore with the relief and relaxation which spring from this recognition" (III/4,552). The rest can only be obtained from God as a matter of pure receiving and establishing instead of endless toil.

56. Freedom in Limitation

Barth completes the last part of volume three by providing some pillars to the fence of freedom that he has spoken at length about. He asserts that God has set a limit of birth and death for his creatures to carry out God's command in the free act of obedience.

"Even in this limitation," Barth says, "therefore, man is summoned to the freedom of obedience to God's command" (III/4, 565). This limitation ought to be perceived as a unique opportunity from God. He indicates that we repeatedly point to the fact that in Christ, God has entered the limitations of birth and death.

Gearing further on the command of God, Barth progresses with vocation in defining it "(. . .) as confronting and corresponding to the divine calling" (III/4, 599). The divine-human confrontation elevates human conditions of life to work in obedience to God's command. In other words, humans find themselves in a vocation instead of choosing one for themselves. It is only in this situation that the full usefulness of humans is accomplished. Thus, in all vocations, irrespective of differences, we all aim for justice in our respective regions.

In conclusion, he uncovers the theme of creaturely honor within the limitation of freedom. He affirms that God clothes a human with honor and glory as we express our willingness to participate in the service. "God alone is competent to decide his dignity and worth (. . .) It is the freedom of His grace. Man cannot claim his honor from God, and he has no power to secure it" (III/4, 678). Therefore, the honor of human beings is nothing but a reflection of God's honor that has dawned upon us in Jesus Christ.

The Doctrine of Reconciliation
(Vol. IV.1)

Chapter 13

The Subject-Matter and Problems of the Doctrine of Reconciliation

57. The Work of God the Reconciler

Barth commences the fourth volume by establishing that humans, by rejecting God, have ruined themselves, so Jesus Christ takes on this humanity as his cause in carrying them to their goal. He proposes that "God with us" is the core value of the Christian message and a decisive statement for the Christian community. "God with us means," Barth writes, "God with the man for whom salvation is intended and ordained as such, as the one who is created, preserved and over-ruled by God as man."[1] In other words, God has made himself the fulfillment of the redemptive will. This assertion is the kernel of Christian faith, hope, and love.

Reconciliation is the fulfillment of the covenant between God and humanity. It is in Jesus Christ, "God Himself enters in, and becomes man, a man amongst men, in order that He Himself in this man may carry out His will. God Himself lives and acts and speaks and suffers and triumphs for all men as this one man" (IV/1, 35). This is the work of atonement in Jesus Christ, revealing God's heart as one who goes beyond the far country to reach humanity with

---

1. Barth, *Church Dogmatics* IV/1, 9; hereafter cited as IV/1.

free grace. He identifies an inseparable relationship between grace and gratitude as they "(. . .) belong together like heaven and earth. Grace evokes gratitude like the voice an echo. Gratitude follows grace like thunder lightning" (IV.1, 41). However, grace can only be received as a gift and can never be recalled.

58. The Doctrine of Reconciliation (Survey)

Jesus Christ is the true reconciler who humbles and yet exalts and stands as "(. . .) the guarantor and witness of our atonement" (IV/1, 79). The atonement is the divine act of God's sovereignty in grace, where God, in reconciliation, crosses the frontier of human situation through the act of power and love. Barth asserts that humans are reconciled to God in Jesus Christ in faith, love, and hope (IV/1, 93). Firstly, faith built on the actuality of Christ and his work assures humans of their justification with ultimate confidence. Secondly, Christian love is love for God that results in our love for our neighbor, as guided by the work of the Holy Spirit. Finally, the hope for eternal life while living with an expectation in the temporal world.

As Barth understands, the atonement fulfills the covenant only through the person of Jesus Christ. "In Him (Jesus Christ)," Barth asserts, "that turning of God to man and conversion of man to God is actuality in the appointed order of the mutual interrelationship (. . .)" (IV/1, 122). He argues for three Christological aspects regarding the entirety of the atonement event, stating that in Jesus Christ, we encounter the true God, true humanity, and observe the humility of God and the exaltation of humanity in the process of reconciliation. "We have to develop the whole doctrine of reconciliation in accordance with our Christology (. . .) The Christology is the key to the whole" (IV.1, 138).

In the light of reconciliation, Barth explores the concept of sin not merely as an evil but as a breach of the covenant. This negation contradicts Christ's reconciliation, resulting in sinful humanity without hope. Christ's birth, death, and resurrection uphold the work of atonement as a once-for-all event. Thus, "faith lives by its object, love by its basis, hope by its surety. Jesus Christ by the Holy Spirit is this object, and basis and surety" (IV/1, 154). In addition, reconciliation is primarily the work of the community, and only then is it the work of individual Christians.

Chapter 14

Jesus Christ, the Lord as Servant

59. The Obedience of the Son of God

The atonement of Christ is actualized and revealed in the history of God and humanity. "The Word," Barth insists, "did not simply become any 'flesh,' any man humbled and suffering. It became Jewish flesh (. . .) The New Testament witness of Jesus the Christ, the Son of God, stands on the soil of the Old Testament and cannot be separated from it" (IV/1, 166). Through this soil, God took our sufferings upon himself by placing himself on the cross of Golgotha, which is "the last word of an old history and the first word of a new." In this act, God remained God despite humiliation without any subtraction or weakening because "(. . .) He did not do it by ceasing to be who He is (. . .) He never became a stranger to Himself" (IV/1, 180). It is on this fact that the atonement is firmly grounded.

The subject of Christian faith and confession is that God in Jesus Christ, along with the Holy Spirit, in mutual fellowship, gave himself to this world as the Reconciler. "But the grace of God," Barth voices, "is not a cheap grace. It costs God dear enough to give this answer, to send His Son as the Savior of the world" (IV/1, 216). He conceptually understands that the essence and root of all sin can be noticed in humans' claim to be their own judge. In his freedom, God chose to judge humanity through his Son. "That is how God has actually judged in Jesus Christ. And that is why He humbled Himself. That is why He went into the far country as the obedient Son of the Father (. . .) He judged, and it was the Judge who was judged, who let Himself be judged." (IV/1, 222). In other words, God, the judge, has rendered judgment upon himself in Jesus Christ by taking our place.

Here, Barth gives significant insight into reconciliation by voicing that Christ is not only 'with us' but also 'for us' in the order of redemption. Indeed, he places God being 'for us' in a higher stance than being 'with us.' He expounds on Jesus being 'for us' in the following ways:

1. Jesus Christ, in being 'for us,' took our place as our Judge in a once-for-all establishment.
2. Jesus Christ was and is 'for us' as he took the place of us as the sinner. So "all our other sins, both small and great, derive ultimately from this source" (IV/1, 235).
3. Jesus suffered, was crucified, and died 'for us.' Because "(. . .) man can do nothing to help himself. That God has intervened in person is the good news of Good Friday" (IV/1, 251).
4. In being 'for us,' Jesus Christ, the Son of God, spoke into world history, and it became world history.

It is noteworthy to observe Barth's emphasis on 'God—for us' over 'God—with us.' He does not undermine the concept of 'with us'; instead, he identifies a more significant redemptive act in Christ's eternal nature of being 'for us,' which cannot be limited to Christ being 'with us' in a historical context. And in history, we see the theology of the cross as central to the doctrine of reconciliation.

And in reconciliation, we see God speaking, suffering, and walking through death in Christ. He affirms that the resurrection of Christ actualizes his death on the cross as the word spoken to humanity of every age that is "acceptably enough for all" (IV/1, 317). "The verdict of God," Barth states, "pronounced in His resurrection tells us that He not only was and is but also will be not only at the end of times, but as Himself the end of time" (IV/1, 324). Barth further identifies the death and resurrection as:

1. The act of God.
2. The act in relation to the crucifixion.
3. Death is connected to the first and final Parousia.

The death and resurrection of Christ ought to be seen as one event and yet a differentiated event, where the death of Christ is accentuated with human will and activity, while the resurrection from the dead is an exclusive act of God. He then cautions that this pure divine revelation cannot be called for further questioning.

60. The Pride and Fall of Man

In discussing the doctrine of sin, Barth proposes that we begin our inquiry into the knowledge of sin in the light of Jesus Christ, who precedes the knowledge of sin. Barth argues, "(. . .) knowledge of real sin takes place in the knowledge of Jesus Christ (. . .)" through his self-offering into death and resurrection, "He has revealed and continually reveals Him as this one who is judged and put to death (. . .)" (IV/1, 390). He also observes that the Old Testament establishes the norm of God's covenant of grace with the Israelite community; in the New Testament, it is through the person and work of Jesus Christ. The norm of covenantal grace forms the center and substance for coherently interpreting the Scriptures.

Barth inquires about the scope of our obedience to Christ and knowledge of sin in the light of Jesus Christ through the following points:

1. The existence of Jesus Christ brings us to the unequivocal understanding of sin in its pure form.
2. Only in the suffering of Jesus Christ are we disclosed to the reality of sin and its sinfulness.

3. "It is again Jesus Christ in whose existence sin is revealed, not only in its actuality and sinfulness, but as the truth of all human being and activity" (IV/1, 403).
4. In Jesus Christ, we arrive at the finality of sin.

In other words, the complete knowledge of sin can only be attained in Christ, who dealt with and conquered sin in the crucifixion and resurrection.

In his discourse on the nature of sin, Barth writes, "(. . .) Sin in its unity and totality is always pride (. . .)" (IV/1, 413). In this pride, humans cease to be humans when they long to be exalted on par with God and to be like God. According to Barth, the self-exaltation of human beings can be attributed to the following reasons:

1. Due to self-alienation.
2. Humans claim to be their own source and standard for achieving their desires.
3. Humans aspire to be the God who is for themselves.

In other words, evil camouflages itself as an exalted virtue. The Word of God is the only hope that sheds light on evil and also guides us to Christ, who "(. . .) by taking our place, by unreservedly allowing that God is in the right against Himself-Himself as the bearer of our guilt" (IV/1, 445). Therefore, salvation is a gift of God that can only be received through Christ in our helplessness.

Barth drives the argument to the fallen state of humans in affirming that human beings have fallen to the place where "(. . .) God who does not and cannot fall has humbled Himself for him in Jesus Christ" (IV/1, 478). He perceives this fallenness as a "vacuum of nothingness" in the world from which God created good by addressing the human beings in the fallen state with a reconciling 'Yes.' Unfortunately, the human response to God's grace is "(. . .) not with a corresponding thankfulness, but in one or many forms of his wretched pride" (IV/1, 489). Indeed, the core of the human heart is evil, corruption, pride, and constantly tossing back and forth in the circle of sin.

On the same lines, Barth ventures into the inner circle of sin in inquiring about the original sin, tracing back to Adam through Paul's conception of sin. He recounts the biblical tradition of sin, which ascribes it to Adam as the representative of the sinful human race. Still, he makes a clear distinction in asserting that Adam's sin is not a fate but a truth concerning humanity. In other words, Adam represents the actuality of the human possibility of sin, which has undoubtedly affected human history.

61. The Justification of Man

Barth finds the root of justification in the event of the death of Jesus Christ. He observes God's judgment with a twofold sense: negatively, it is the consuming fire and wrath on the corrupt, while positively, God has turned to humans in goodness, mercy, and grace. In this process, human mischief is not left for themselves but is directed towards this gracious God. Here, Barth uses an analogy of two hands of God: where "(. . .) on the left hand it is the case that God judges man and his wrong in all seriousness, that He destroys him genuinely and truly and altogether, that this man has actually to die (. . .)" While "(. . .) on the right hand it is the case that God accepts His creature and elect genuinely and truly and altogether, that the faithfulness which He displays to him (. . .)" (IV/1, 542). Thus, justification cannot be comprehended with mere subjective human experience but should be embraced as a mystery in humility, acknowledging that in Christ, the removal of sin and the restoration of marred dignity have been accomplished.

In the virtue of human pardon, Barth clarifies three things:

1. It can only be God's sentence to humans.
2. It can only be received as a Word of God addressed to humanity.
3. It has total authority and is not partial.

"The divine pardon," Barth writes, "does not burst into man's willingness but his unwillingness. Man will always be a miracle and a puzzle to himself as he breaks out in this way" (IV/1, 576). Under this judgment, a human is always a sinner, yet justified.

He finally ventures into the aspect of justification by faith, defining faith as "wholly and utterly humility" (IV/1, 618). It is not a self-chosen humility based on mere thinking, knowing, trusting, but a free decision in obedience. Drawing from Luther's concept of *sola fide*, Barth grounds faith in love by recounting it as living and active. He establishes that Jesus Christ is the only hope for human justification. In other words, faith ceases to be faith if not in Jesus Christ. Therefore, justification by faith is the liberation for humanity, where God has come to humans rather than vice versa.

62. The Holy Spirit and the Gathering of the Christian Community

Barth begins this section with a quick recap of the doctrine of reconciliation, which can be better understood in the following diagram.

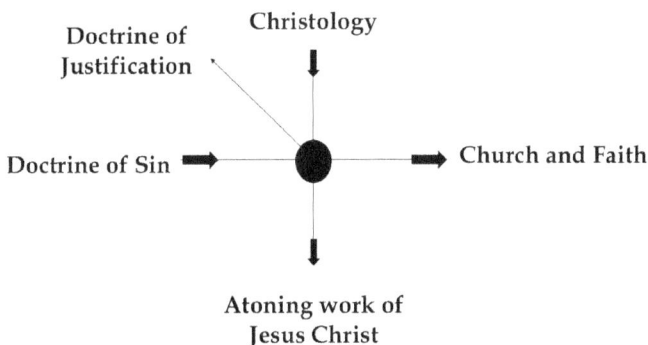

The vertical line represents the Christological aspect that finds its fulfillment in Christ's atoning work. The horizontal line illustrates the doctrine of sin, which culminates in the church and faith. Both lines intersect in the doctrine of justification, resulting in assurance and hope for humanity.

Barth reemphasizes that Jesus Christ is the center of Christian faith and confession. "We can move only within the circle," Barth writes, "that they are founded by the Holy Spirit and therefore that they must be continually refounded by Him (. . .)" (IV/1, 647). The Christian community, by and large, is called to prepare faith as its primary goal, and the church, as a community of Christ's body, is continually awakened by the power of the Holy Spirit to pursue this goal. And the unity of the church finds its ground in the "nature of Israel as the people of Jesus Christ is that of the church" (IV/1, 689). In other words, Barth traces the Christ event and the church as fulfilling Israel's history.

He further asserts that the church ought to be catholic, or it is not the church at all. And the apostles, who are counted as the rock of the church, are not lords of the church; instead, Jesus makes use of them. "Their authority, power and mission consists in the fact that He does this. In this they are the rock on which He builds His Church" (IV/1, 718–719). The church is built on the authority of the Bible as the source and norm, which he calls "the Scripture principle." And the church's timeline lies between Christ's first and second coming (Parousia). Barth perceives that the church, on the one hand, is the community of God who wills all humans to be saved and come into the knowledge of the truth. On the other hand, "(. . .) it is made sure only in the awakening and sustaining of its faith by One who is able to do this" (IV/1, 733). Thus, the church serves as a transformative entity that operates as a community grounded in faith, maintaining the proper relationship between Christ and the world.

63. The Holy Spirit and Christian Faith

Barth begins the section by examining the relationship between the Christian faith and the Holy Spirit. Faith, for Barth, is a subjective realization that aims to follow its object. As opposed to the traditional understanding, he argues that "in faith man ceases to be in control (. . .) In faith man is no longer in control at his centre. Or rather, at his centre, he is outside himself and therefore in control" of Jesus Christ who is the object of faith (IV/1, 743). "Faith is the simple discovery," Barth says, "of the child which finds itself in the father's house and on the mother's lap" (IV/1, 748). Yet, this faith is a mysterious circle, primarily enclosed by Christ's actions and human existence.

Along with love and hope, Barth affirms that faith "(. . .) is the most inward and central and decisive act of his heart (. . .)" (IV/1, 757). He expresses that faith consists of three aspects: acknowledgement, recognition, and confession:

1. We realize and acknowledge that Christ has conquered us for himself over the proclamation of the church.
2. Faith is a recognition in obedience and cognizance.
3. Christian faith is inseparable from confession.

"A Christian," Barth notes, "who simply acknowledges and recognises without confessing is not a Christian" (IV/1, 776). Thus, a confessing Christian is the one who communicates the confession to her neighbor, resulting in a confessing community.

The Doctrine of Reconciliation
(Vol. IV.2)

Chapter 15

Jesus Christ, the Servant as Lord

64. The Exaltation of the Son of Man

Barth begins this section by reestablishing the premise that the reconciliation of the world with God has taken place only in Jesus Christ, placing humans at the center of this event.

> The atonement as it took place in Jesus Christ is the one inclusive event of this going out of the Son of God and coming in of the Son of Man (. . .) It was God who went into the far country, and it is man who returns home. Both took place in the one Jesus Christ. It is not therefore a matter of two different and successive actions, but of a single action (. . .)[1]

In this action, Jesus is the true God and true man simultaneously. He asserts that we cannot limit Christ to the high priestly office, but that he is also to be explored simultaneously as exercising his office as a servant. His deity and humanity should be perceived as a unified event in the reconciliation, not as separate. In the two natures of Christ, the divine nature is imparted over the human nature, while the human nature embraces the divine essence. The divine essence is above the human one, and works mutually in a

---

1. Barth, *Church Dogmatics* IV/2, 21; hereafter cited as IV/2.

genuine relationship. He further examines the role of the Holy Spirit in the reconciling work of Christ, who assumes a primary role in bearing witness to Jesus Christ and his self-revelation (IV/2, 129). In sum, the origin, content, and purpose of reconciliation are indeed Jesus Christ, which was carried into the "Easter-event as revelation" (IV/2, 146).

Barth introduces the concept of the royal man in the context of a strange destiny, portraying him as one who was forgotten, despised, and discounted by humans. This is so because "(. . .) He ignored all those who are high and mighty and wealthy in the world in favour of the weak and meek and lowly" (IV/2, 168). In this fashion, God engages with the nothingness that aims at human destruction. "Faith in Him (Jesus Christ)," Barth voices, "is faith in the Crucified. Love for Him is love for the Crucified (. . .) The great light of Easter is for it the light of Good Friday penetrating the darkness" (IV/2, 250).

As a concluding element of this section, Barth advances his argument towards Christ, who is depicted as the royal man within whose authority is the life of a Christian community, and the essence of Christian love is sustained. In other words, God penetrates humanity in Christ through the work of grace by reaching the goal of regeneration and conversion of humankind through the royal power of resurrection. Thus, the reconciliation between God and humanity is revealed in Jesus Christ's resurrection from death.

However, the mystery of the royal man, i.e., Christ, is crowned with the shame of the cross. But the good news lies in easter, where Barth asserts, "The Christian community is the Easter community. Our preaching is Easter preaching, our hymns are Easter hymns, our faith is an Easter faith" (IV/2, 355). This implies that the Christian faith is a living faith that receives its direction from the Holy Spirit, and the Christian community lives under this guidance, shaped by it (IV/2, 362).

65. The Sloth and Misery of Man

Humans, as self-enclosed beings, are subject to anxiety and foolishness, which eventually leads to their death. This misery of humans, as Barth writes, "(. . .) is in contradiction to his nature, so that when he does it, he is a stranger to himself." (IV/2, 393). In other words, humans, by definition, are good creatures, but are capable of estranging themselves from their nature. Barth identifies this sinful nature as the sloth of humans. In light of this situation, Jesus Christ presents himself as an establishing grace within the framework of reconciling grace.

He further examines human sloth as a manifestation of sin that leads to a failure to accept God. In light of this situation, Barth promptly delineates four aspects of the mortal refusal of the freedom that was promised in Jesus Christ:

1. The eternal Word became flesh, which deals with the economy of human stupidity.
2. The Word has become the power of grace in the existence of the human community.
3. Through the existence of human Jesus, we deal with the true and authentic human life.
4. Through Jesus, we exercise royal freedom in acknowledging that he gave his life in reconciling God and humans (IV/2, 467).

He further ventures into the misery of humans by defining it as "the situation which we create (in our stupidity and inhumanity and vagabondage and discontent) is the misery of man in the sense of his exile as the sum of human woe" (IV/2, 483). In humility, Jesus reaches out to this humanity, taking our misery upon himself and making us new. In other words, "in Jesus we are all back home again" (IV/2, 488). Thus, Barth views freedom as essential for genuine fellowship between God and humans, contrasting it with the human sloth and misery that neglects this freedom.

66. The Sanctification of Man

The divine right over humans does not limit itself to justification but perpetuates sanctification in an indissoluble unity. In other words, justification and sanctification are two distinct moments that coexist in the one act of reconciliation (IV/2, 503). The act of reconciliation was made possible by God's holiness, by crossing the infinite distance that separates the holy God from sinful humanity. We cannot claim or credit sanctification for ourselves because "their (humans) sanctification is originally and properly His and not theirs" (IV/2, 514).

Barth seconded Calvin's doctrine of *participatio Christi*, in which humans participate in the sanctity of Jesus Christ through the Holy Spirit. In other words, the process of sanctification is facilitated through the Holy Spirit, either in an individual's life or within a community. Similarly, this process can be observed even in the discipleship where "(. . .) the substance of the call in the power of which Jesus makes men His saints (. . .) The call issued by Jesus is a call to discipleship" (IV/2, 533). This call includes four key aspects:

1. The call discloses and reveals Jesus to humanity by sanctifying them and summoning them as witnesses in the world.
2. The call binds a person to follow the one who gives it.
3. The call ought to be received in obedience to faith in Jesus.
4. The call is exercised in self-denial (IV/2, 543).

Barth affirms that the sanctified are those who are awakened for a counter-movement of past life. On the one hand, the awakening or renewal is never without a fellow human; on the other, it "(. . .) is not the affair of these individual moments; it is the affair of the totality of the whole life-movement of man" (IV/2, 566). He upholds Luther's dictum of *simul (totus) iustus, simul (totus) peccator* as the dying of the old and rising of the new person. Finally, he reemphasizes, "(. . .) what Calvin called the *participatio*

Christi, making it the ultimate foundation of his whole doctrine of sanctification" (IV/2, 581).

And the works of the sanctified point to the Trinitarian God as the commencement of the good works. In sum, "(. . .) the good work of God which alone makes possible the good works of man" (IV/2, 591). He voices that the cross is the essential and provisional existence of the fellowship between Christ and the Christian in the journey of sanctification. Hence, he concludes the (German) paragraph with two key observations: the self-sought suffering has nothing to add to human sanctification, and it is in the dignity of the cross that we find "(. . .) the Christian existence and all sanctification" (IV/2, 613).

67. The Holy Spirit and the Upbuilding of the Christian Community

Barth identifies the Holy Spirit as "the quickening power" through which Jesus builds his body, the church. The Christian community, i.e., the church, is built on the sanctifying work of the Spirit to which Christ gives marginal control. In other words, God works towards the upbuilding of the community through the mutual working of Jesus and his Spirit as one God. "Thus the only content of the Holy Spirit is Jesus; His only work is His provisional revelation (. . .) Where the man Jesus attests Himself in the power of the Spirit of God (. . .)" (IV/2, 654). We notice that Barth's pneumatology is undoubtedly powered and guided by Christology.

He furthers the inquiry by recognizing the perpetual danger of the Christian community. He posits the danger of sacralization downplaying the Gospel as "(. . .) a pseudo-sacred law erected and proclaimed on the supposed basis of the Gospel" and makes "sacralization as well as secularisation" as "the end of the community" (IV/2, 670). In contrast, the Scripture principle achieves the task of upholding the community by itself. However, Barth articulates that the role of Scripture is to serve as an instrument that supports the church through the power of Jesus Christ. In other words, "He (Jesus Christ) verifies Scripture simply by the fact that He is its content; that as it is read and heard He Himself is present to speak and act as the living Lord of the church" (IV/2, 675). It is noteworthy that Barth again places Jesus Christ at the center of the Scripture, and the Scriptures point to him as the living Word.

In the context of the order of the community, He voices that the canon law cannot be derived from any other source besides "(. . .) a christologico-ecclesiology concept of the community. The community as Jesus Christ is—He who is the Lord of the human communion of saints, the Head of his body, which is the earthly-historical form of His own existence" (IV/2, 679). The community can be juxtaposed with the state during uncertain periods in external aspects. Still, the community must confess its ground as to be spiritual, and it is from this center that the community stands in relation to its civil authority. Internally, the law and order of the community can never be limited to a few priests but to "the universal priesthood of all believers." Hence, the church exists for a divine service that needs perpetual reconsideration.

Barth's arguments further emphasize the fellowship of baptism in the community. He identifies that the community's public life involves "(. . .) not only of confession and baptism and the Lord's Supper, but also of prayer" (IV/2, 706). Thus, through these aspects of fellowship, we discern the true law of the church and find its proclamation "as Gospel proclaiming the Gospel" (IV/2, 726).

68. The Holy Spirit and Christian Love

Barth understands that a true human has entered the sphere of Jesus Christ through the quickening power of the Holy Spirit as opposed to coerced discipleship. The quickening process encompasses justification and sanctification as two distinct yet complementary divine actions. A Christian, as an individual, can never be separated from the community; i.e., they can never resist self-giving love. But this self-giving is not self-denial; instead, it is self-assertion where "(. . .) the loving subject finds itself summoned and stirred to turn to another" (IV.2, 734). For Barth, self-giving is never an act of exhaustion, but rather a living in a mutual exchange of love.

He explores the theme of agape love in contrast to eros love; the former is given without any expectations in return, while the latter opposes human nature as a denial of humanity. For Barth, the two forms of love operate in a see-saw dynamics, where one rises and the other sinks, and vice versa. He argues that human love can only be seen as a contingent factor of divine love for God. "God is" and "God loves" are inseparable and stand in mutual affirmation, where the eternal love "(. . .) precedes our love in this majesty, it is the firm basis of our love" (IV/2, 755). In other words, trinitarian love is the basis of all other love, as he defines it as electing, purifying, and creative love.

In discussing the act of love, "we have to do with nothing more nor less," Barth writes, "than a revelation of the real presence of God in Jesus Christ" (IV/2, 785). In the act of love, humans subordinate themselves to the will and command of God. And it is by the Holy Spirit that humans are liberated to receive love and love in return. This love transforms the old creature into the new one in Christ. Therefore, the Christian covenant community finds its promise only in the form of love accompanied by faith and hope.

The Doctrine of Reconciliation
(Vol. IV.3, First Half)

Chapter 16

Jesus Christ, the True Witness

69. The Glory of the Mediator

Barth establishes the reconciling work of God as the actualization of the covenant, where humans are graciously elected through the divine "yes" over the human "no." He observes an inseparable relationship between revelation and reconciliation, stating that revelation comes to us as the revelation of reconciliation. "It (revelation) takes place as reconciliation takes place; as it has in it its origin, content and subject; as reconciliation is revealed and reveals itself in it."[1] Both are intrinsic to their past, present, and future occurrences. God has reconciled with us, and as a result, he has revealed himself to us. Indeed, revelation finds its origin in reconciliation.

The movement of reconciliation history needs to be understood in the context of the Israelites' history, which culminates in the New Testament community. This movement is ascribed to no other than Jesus Christ, as attested in the Scriptures. "In the life of Jesus Christ," Barth writes, "there takes place, with the establishment of the new order, the reconstitution of the old" (IV/3, 43). "In all history (Jesus Christ) there is some mystery. But it is only in the history of Israel that this mystery announces itself" (IV/3, 66). It is by these means that we perceive Christ in Word and prophecy.

---

1. Barth, *Church Dogmatics* IV/3, 9; hereafter cited as IV/3.

Barth persuades his argument that Jesus Christ is the only Word of God, and there was, or is, no other Word spoken by God.

And one needs to obey this Word in life and death. "But we have every cause to keep to the fact that He is faithful, and that in Jesus Christ we have His total and unique and therefore authentic revelation, the Word in which He does full justice both to Himself and us" (IV/3, 100). Here, Barth voices a reciprocal interpretation of community and Christ by stating that the Christian community stands in faithful witness to Scripture as long as they align themselves with the one Word, i.e., Jesus Christ. On the one hand, the community presents Christ through Scriptures; on the other hand, Christ, in turn, sets the community on its correct path of proclamation (IV/3, 114). Thus, the prophetic work of Jesus Christ is an event of reconciliation between God and humans. "It is in Him (Jesus Christ)," Barth states, "as this Reconciler of the world that the community believes. It is He as this Reconciler who is the theme of its proclamation. It derives from His resurrection in which He was manifested as this Reconciler of the world" (IV/3, 116).

He observes three characteristics of the Word of God in the following ways:

1. The Word of God binds itself in certainty in humans as they hear it.
2. The Word of God comes in its totality and needs no further addition or division.
3. The Word of God gives and receives itself in the prophetic event of Jesus Christ.

In other words, the Word (Scripture) draws us together in communion with Jesus Christ.

Barth progresses to a new section in the theme of the prophetic work of Christ, focusing on the challenge of *Christus Victor*, i.e., 'Christ is Victor.' He argues that in the light of hope for the future, the human situation can be better perceived through the lens of Christus victor. All salvation history is the *totus Christus,* which is the Christus victor.

> Jesus is Victor already both in the beginning of His prophecy and in its present course right up to the present day. He suffers no defeats. He is never at a halt or in retreat. But He is not yet at the conclusion of this warfare which, so far as He and His action are concerned, is always victorious" (IV/3, 262).

For Barth, the work of Christ in word and prophecy is always victorious and nothing other. He observes the superiority of Christ in relation to the victory of his prophetic work in three points:

1. The Word of God is superior to all other words.
2. The Word of God is superior as it is mediated and accomplished through the act of the Word itself.
3. As the superior Word of prophecy, it is directed to the real human.

In conclusion, Barth argues that we ought to comprehend the episodes of resurrection, the outpouring of the Spirit, and the second coming of Christ as one and the same event. However, he acknowledges the specific emphasis of each episode in the broader theme of reconciliation. The resurrection is seen as "divine yea and amen," pointing to the future hope of salvation that eventuates in the Parousia. And the Spirit who is promised is the content of the promise yet to be fulfilled. Then what about the unbelievers? Barth affirms, "Their blindness and deafness still stand like a dam against the surging and mounting stream. But the stream is too strong and the dam too weak for us to be able reasonably to expect anything but the collapse of the dam and the onrush of the waters. In this sense Jesus Christ is the hope even of these non-Christians" (IV/3, 356). The analogy of a dam and a stream signifies an unwavering endeavor towards reconciliation, where we find an assured hope for the hopeless.

THE DOCTRINE OF RECONCILIATION (VOL. IV.3, FIRST HALF)

70. The Falsehood and Condemnation of Man

Barth contends that the falsehood of humans is a counterstrike to grace in its trajectory toward nothingness. God in Christ encounters us as the faithful witness in the once-for-all movement. God is not bound to this reconciliation, but chose to live with it. And the essence of God is declared in the reconciling work of Jesus in the sphere of history. In contrast, the falsehood of human stands, resisting the prophetic work of Jesus Christ. This resistance is evident when a person tries to dominate and champion the truth in an attempt to silence it. This nature of human sin is observed in the maturity of falsehood. However, all these human efforts are ultimately destroyed when encountered by Jesus Christ.

Humanity stands condemned by God. "To be condemned is to be (. . .) judged by God" (IV/3, 462). In falsehood, humans are coerced to live in lies and are constantly distorted to the extent that they are rejected and lost. Amid this scenario, Barth ends this section with a hope for the human falsehood in two points:

1. He hopes for an unexpected work of grace that can be received only as a gift.
2. Musing on such a possibility, we are advised to hope and pray.

It is evident that Barth, who has consistently viewed his theology from the prism of Jesus Christ, the Word, finds it challenging to relinquish any resisting floodgates that can effectively withstand the infinite ocean of God's love and mercy.

The Doctrine of Reconciliation (Vol. IV.3, Second Half)

71. The Vocation of Man

The sign of vocation, like justification and sanctification, should be understood as a "continual confirmation" in a person's life. This vocation finds its foundation in the election, where God, in Christ, has elected all humans through an act of free grace that required no cooperation on the part of humans. He further asserts that the process of vocation goes beyond Luther's statement of the Holy Spirit not only calling to enlighten and sanctify, but also as the origin, author, and acting subject of vocation. "But even the worst sin," Barth writes, "of the Christian cannot alter the totality of what befalls him in the process of his vocation."[1]

The theme of vocation can be observed directly through God's direct mediation by the Holy Spirit, and indirectly through the ministry of the prophets, apostles, and their successors. He argues that the doctrine of vocation is one of the central aspects of Christian faith, where the one (Jesus Christ) who calls us is also the one who confronts and within it, and through it in us. Thus, the vocation as external and internal, "(. . .) in its once-for-allness His calling is continuous, yet continuous without denying its once-for-allness" (IV/3, 520). Vocation constitutes another recurring

---

1. Barth, *Church Dogmatics* IV/3, 508; hereafter cited as IV/3.

theme within Barth's explicit dialectical thinking pattern in his theological framework.

Vocation is what sets a Christian apart from others. A Christian in Christ means that a person is attested with the vocation. The goal of the vocation can be perceived as fellowship with Jesus Christ, "(. . .) who thus lives in the knowledge that he does not belong to himself but to his Lord" (IV/3, 536). And the Holy Spirit carries out the vocation process of declaring the union between a Christian and Jesus Christ. As recipients of grace, we are illumined and born again to live in obedience to the command. The command to be his witness is the task for the Christian. "The essence of their vocation," Barth states, "is that God makes them His witnesses" (IV/3, 575). In other words, "(. . .) the self-giving of Christ to the Christian and the Christian to Christ is the goal of vocation, the true being of the Christian" (IV/3, 594). Indeed, in Barth's view, there can never be a Christian without vocation.

However, Barth sees a concern for Christians as they are exposed to suffering and affliction. Indeed, real Christians, he affirms, are those who are oppressed by the world. "In every form the really oppressive feature is the defamation and ostracism to which the Christian is exposed as a witness (. . .) This is the affliction of the Christian" (IV/3, 624). Conversely, Christian liberation constitutes a distinctive grace that transcends mere concepts of freedom or release, embodying a redemption that emphasizes responsibility, inscribed in the heart as a gesture of gratitude. Indeed, liberation transitions us from anxiety to prayer, culminating in the Christian's engagement with the world and bearing witness to Christ in the world.

72. The Holy Spirit and the Sending of the Christian Community

After a careful discourse on vocation, Barth continues the theme by stating that the Christian community is called to be a living community of the Lord Jesus Christ. But this community is challenged and tossed with a confusion on two fronts: "(. . .) the good creation of God and therefore the creaturely reality elected and willed by Him on the one side, and its negation as rejected by God and therefore that which is intrinsically impossible on the other" (IV/3, 696). Amid this dialectical confusion, the community still persists in the providence of God.

"It is the grace of God," Barth writes, "the name of Jesus Christ" as the "instrument or vehicle used by God in addressing His grace to the world" (IV/3, 710). In faith, the community acknowledges that the transformation of the world occurred during the Christ event, who, as the invisible being, lives and guides the community on its path through the Holy Spirit. The community exists for God, and in this existence, it finds its place in and for the world. He states the characteristics of a true community as follows:

1. The fellowship in Christ helps the community to understand the origin and purpose of the world.
2. The community is set on the task to live in solidarity with the world.
3. The community finds its obligation to the world for which Christ suffered and offered himself to it.

In addressing the presuppositions concerning the Christian community, the individual affirms that the Holy Spirit liberates and sustains the community, while the origin and destiny of the community are perfected and ultimately brought to a definitive conclusion in a manner analogous to the process observed in Jesus Christ.

The Christian community is not randomly placed in the world but firmly set on a specific task. This task is entrusted to the community by Christ, made known through the enlightenment of the Holy Spirit. We also notice that this community may appear distinct from the rest of humanity, yet it remains unified. He makes three statements demonstrating the relationship between Christ, the church, and the world.

THE DOCTRINE OF RECONCILIATION (VOL. IV.3, SECOND HALF)

1. "The world would be lost without Jesus Christ and His Word and work.
2. The world would not necessarily be lost if there were no Church.
3. The church would be lost if it had no counterpart in the world" (IV/3, 836).

Thus, the church and world live in abiding distinction through the mediating power of the Holy Spirit.

Finally, Barth grounds the ministry of the community as "(. . .) very definite, and therefore limited, but also full of promise" (IV/3, 830). Firstly, the definiteness of the ministry rests on the community's firm relationship with the world. Secondly, the limitation can be seen as its subordination to the specific command of God without digression (IV/3, 833). Thirdly, the promise of the ministry is assured with protection and sustenance. He asserts that this ministry serves as the community's witness in proclaiming and declaring the gospel, which takes practical form in evangelism. This ministry can be further observed in various forms, including the office of praise within the community, which is expressed through singing. "Singing" for Barth, "(. . .) is the highest form of human expression (. . .)" that binds the community (IV/3, 866). The other forms of ministry include: proclamation, exposition of Scripture, instruction, sending out to the nations, prayer as thanksgiving and intercession, care of souls, service, prophetic witness, fellowship through baptism, and the Lord's Supper, among others.

73. The Holy Spirit and Christian Hope

In answering the question of the possibility of Christian witness, Barth asserts that our witness in Jesus Christ leads a person to strive towards a future in hope. And this hope is not in twilight but explicitly the hope of promising salvation that flows seamlessly from the righteousness and grace of God. He explores Christian hope as living between the *then* of resurrection and the *now* of

Pentecost. The two events live in inseparable unity and express the two different forms of the same Parousia of Jesus Christ (IV/3, 911). Barth reemphasizes, in line with the doctrine of election, that Jesus Christ is both the subject and object of hope, through which a Christian is assured of faith and love.

The Christian hope, as Barth understands, carries a negative connotation on one hand, implying a life of obscurity and fear. On the other hand, the positive connotation is associated with the Parousia and the completion of prophetic work. "For this reason," Barth writes, "the problems of faith, love and hope must certainly be raised and answered as personal or 'existential' questions of the Christian individual" (IV/3, 930). However, life in faith, hope, and love is not possible only through human acts, but by God's act, who works mysteriously. Thus, God himself embodies the Holy Spirit, who ignites hope that achieves its ultimate freedom when firmly anchored in Jesus Christ.

The Doctrine of Reconciliation (Vol. IV.4—Fragment)

The Foundation of the Christian Life

Barth commences this section by inquiring about the means by which one might be called a Christian. He expounds on the divine possibility of a "magical infusion of spiritual powers" through which a person's whole being is restored to God.[1] He establishes that "Jesus Christ is the One elected from eternity to be the Head and Saviour of all men" who through the life, teaching, death, and resurrection has redeemed the humanity, "(. . .) the One who did this for all, the change which took place in His history took place for all" (IV/4, 13). In Christ's history, Christians find their full potential and a share through the mediating work of the Holy Spirit. In other words, it is a passive participation on the human side as Christ takes their place as the liberator.

The history of Christ does not disdain a person's history, but it becomes a new history. "God wills," Barth writes, "in this history and with its manifestation is that all men should be saved, that they should be brought subjectively to the truth (1 Tim. 2:4), and that in this knowledge they should be freed for faithfulness to Him" (IV/4, 29).

Barth further develops the argument by venturing into the doctrine of baptism. He affirms baptism in two forms: baptism of

---

1. Barth, *Church Dogmatics* IV/4, 4; hereafter cited as IV/4.

the Spirit and baptism with water. The Christian journey sparks with an active Word, i.e., baptism of the Spirit, which leads to baptism with water. In other words, the Spirit baptism finds its completion in the future event of water baptism. Regarding water baptism, Barth asserts that the New Testament provides quantitative data on the practice of baptism. Subsequently, he proceeds to discuss its basis, goal, and meaning.

The basis of baptism can be firmly established not on the command and commission of teaching baptism but on the baptism of Jesus, where "(. . .) the particular interest of the event is that it was the exemplary and imperative baptismal event" (IV/4, 53). This event can also be understood as God's work of reconciliation that has occurred through the history of Jesus Christ.

The goal of baptism is God's reconciling work in Jesus Christ through the Holy Spirit. He summarizes that "(. . .) baptism is the human work of basic confession in which the Christian community finds itself associated with those who are newly joining it (. . .) More accurately, it is the confession of the obedience of their faith, the active confession which consists as such in a washing of the candidates with water" (IV/4, 73). It is noticeable that for Barth, baptism is undoubtedly a journey of obedience in tandem with the divine commission. In other words, baptism sets a person on the path of obedience to faith.

The meaning of baptism can be perceived as an instrument of God's grace that not only justifies but also sanctifies and calls. The meaning of baptism, states Barth, "(. . .) lies in a strict correlation and a no less strict distinction between the human action as such and the divine action from which it springs, on whose basis it is possible, and towards which it moves" (IV/4, 134). In other words, human action, as understood in terms of obedience and hope in its correlative relation with divine work, constitutes the meaning of baptism.

Barth then moves to the doctrine of infant baptism, countering the reformers' criticism of their teaching and advocacy for infant baptism. He navigates the argument through Luther, Zwingli, and Calvin in questioning the historical normativity and theological significance of the practice of infant baptism. "(. . .) Infant baptism," Barth writes, "is so remarkably vivid a depiction of the free and omnipotent grace of God which is independent of all human thought and will, faith and unbelief" (IV/4, 189). He does not find robust theological or historical arguments to support infant baptism. Finally, he asserts,

> This practice is profoundly irregular. It is true that through the centuries and up to our own time the church has not been destroyed by it (any more than by corrupt preaching or so many other corruptions). But it would be most dangerous—of all arguments for infant baptism this is the worst—to appeal to the fact, or to rely on it, that this practice will not harm it in the future (IV/4, 194).

Barth warns the church that the longstanding tradition of infant baptism may not ensure safety from disaster in the days to come. However, the hope of new life can be acknowledged through the power of Jesus Christ's resurrection, who alone is the community's future. Thus, baptism is the first step into the Christian life, commanded as an act of obedience and prayer, and exercised in freedom, once and for all, and serves as a paradigm for all that follows in the Christian life and work.

Bibliography

Barth, Karl. *Church Dogmatics 1/1*, 2nd ed. Edinburgh: T&T Clark, 1975.
———. *Church Dogmatics 1/2*. Edinburgh: T&T Clark, 1956.
———. *Church Dogmatics 2/1*. Edinburgh: T&T Clark, 1957.
———. *Church Dogmatics 2/2*. Edinburgh: T&T Clark, 1957.
———. *Church Dogmatics 3/1*. Edinburgh: T&T Clark, 1958.
———. *Church Dogmatics 3/2*. Edinburgh: T&T Clark, 1960.
———. *Church Dogmatics 3/3*. Edinburgh: T&T Clark, 1960.
———. *Church Dogmatics 3/4*. Edinburgh: T&T Clark, 1961.
———. *Church Dogmatics 4/1*. Edinburgh: T&T Clark, 1956.
———. *Church Dogmatics 4/2*. Edinburgh: T&T Clark, 1958.
———. *Church Dogmatics 4/3, first half*. Edinburgh: T&T Clark, 1961.
———. *Church Dogmatics 4/3, second half*. Edinburgh: T&T Clark, 1962.
———. *Church Dogmatics 4/4*. Edinburgh: T&T Clark, 1969.